DANCING IN THE FOʊ ıɔ ı ⸝ɔ ʊʜ EVE

Dancing in the Footsteps of Eve *is a beautifully written book about the return of a sense of divinity. Heather Mendel is especially sensitive to the spiritual needs of women. But the real contribution of this book is to offer an intelligent, intimate, and relevant idea of God in a time of confusion and forgetting.*
Thomas Moore, author of *Care of the Soul*

Dancing In The Footsteps of Eve *is a highly original book, an ambitious and creative undertaking. Heather Mendel's scholarship and knowledge of religious writings combine with her deeply felt reflections and enlightened consciousness to illuminate a remarkable personal journey by a woman steeped in Jewish tradition in search of the divine feminine.*
Riane Eisler, author of *The Chalice and The Blade, Sacred Pleasure,* and *The Real Wealth of Nations*

Wisdom in every culture is deemed to be feminine. The Book of Proverbs says it best. Surprise! Surprise! Wisdom is full of delight! Mendel proves this by making even her scholarly research a treat to read. She restores the role of the feminine in an earthy, practical way while at the same time honoring the masculine and intellectual genius of traditional Judaism. In this book the Tree of Life blossoms with joy.
Alice O. Howell, author of *The Dove In the Stone: Finding the Sacred in the Commonplace*

The return of the divine Mother — Hochmah, Shechina, Sophia — heralds the transformation of the human spirit from competing religious tribes to shared explorations of divine consciousness. She comes to us and through us, and every once in a while there is that rare soul among us

i

with the capacity to help awaken us to Her presence. Heather Mendel is one of these souls and Dancing in the Footsteps of Eve *is one of these awakenings. This book is a delight.*

Rabbi Rami Shapiro, author of *The Divine Feminine*

Autobiography, history, theology, midrash, kabbalah and, of course, feminism all seamlessly woven together into a wise and wonderful literary adventure. From ancient tradition to New Age, Heather Mendel sets a banquet table for the 21st century spiritual seeker. This is a beautiful book.

Rabbi Lawrence Kushner, the Emanu-El Scholar at Congregation Emanu-El of San Francisco and author of the novel, *Kabbalah: A Love Story*, and sixteen books on Judaism, Kabbalah, and spirituality.

In this engaging, wide-ranging work, Heather Mendel draws on an astonishing number of sources in her effort to reconcile her deep-rooted Judaism with her vision of a post-patriarchal world in which her feminist convictions flourish. The result is an entrancing vision of an enlarged and revitalized tradition that honors the past in a creative engagement with the challenges of a contemporary world. In the best traditions of Judaism, the author seeks to rescue the holy from the limiting definitions in which we forever attempt to ensnare it. In the process, she offers us a God who does not need defending, a feminism that does not need to be rooted in anger and frustration in order to be vital, and a possible spiritual discipline that daily deepens our appreciation of the world and strengthens our resolve to serve it.

Rev. David Bumbaugh, Minister Emeritus, The Unitarian Church in Summit, NJ and Professor of Ministry, Meadville Lombard and author of *The Education of God and Unitarian Universalism: A Narrative History*

Heather Mendel's "dance" is an archaeology of hope, a vision of feminist values, of egalitarian life and of the interconnections between all beings and with the Earth. It is a re-memory of the Sacred Feminine in Jewish tradition, of an inclusive Divinity, one that is always coming into being. Heather Mendel interprets and celebrates the Sacred Feminine honoring "both our individual uniqueness and spectacular diversity." Although written over many years, Dancing in the Footsteps of Eve *is a prescient meditation on our Oneness, as its publication coincides with the inauguration of President Barak Obama and the spirit of Oneness and community that has, at least at this moment, enveloped the world in a fusion of hope.*

Bettina Aptheker, Professor, Feminist Studies/Jewish Studies, University of California, Santa Cruz and author of *Intimate Politics: How I Grew Up Red, Fought for Free Speech and Became A Feminist Rebel.*

With Dancing in the Footsteps of Eve, *Heather Mendel joins the welcome chorus of feminist scholarship unearthing and reclaiming the Biblical tradition of the divine feminine. Yet, her candid and tender spiritual memoir is told within, and continually dialogues with, the wider context of her own faith community in Judaism. With an ear for both the needs of the beginning inquirer as well as the more theologically sophisticated scholar, Mendel guides us through a careful retrieving of these life-giving feminine threads in the patriarchal fabric of sacred text. Choosing not to discard the original damaged cloth, she guides us in the reweaving and strengthening of our concepts and experiences of the Holy. Her extensive research provides references for those who want to learn more and she offers experiential exercises for those yearning to engage the heart. This is accessible and engaging reading for Jews, Christians and seekers alike, and a helpful guide for both laypeople and clergy leaders in congregations. Mendel reminds us that the re-integration of the marginalized parts of both sacred tradition and self will bring great wholeness and healing to all humankind.*

The Rev. Anne Swallow Gillis, MDiv, MSW, Protestant Minister and Pastoral Counselor

At this time in the evolution of the human family, Dancing in the Footsteps of Eve *is a welcome teaching. It recalls the integrity of feminine wisdom and the innate knowledge that power with is always more effective than power over. This book is a needed reminder of both the revealed and concealed power of the divine feminine.*

Beverly Engel, author of *The Nice Girl Syndrome: Stop Being Manipulated and Abused - and Start Standing Up for Yourself*

The Torah teaches that Eve's name in Hebrew means "Mother of all Living." With her wonderful new book Heather Mendel reminds us that we, the living, are - all of us - still dancing in her footsteps. And what a dance it is. Sun and moon; bride and groom; kashrut and karma: chronos and kairos; ontogeny and phylogeny; the mythical and mystical; anima and animus; God and, of course, Goddess. Enjoy!

Rabbi Mark Sameth, author of *God's Hidden Name Revealed (Reform Judaism)* and *Who is He? He is She, CCAR Journal*

Dancing
in the Footsteps
of Eve

Retrieving The Healing Gift Of The
Sacred Feminine For The Human Family
Through Myth and Mysticism

For my ~~friend~~ Judy.
Welcome to the dance
L'Shalom
Heather Mendel

~~for~~ my landman :‿)

Dancing
in the Footsteps
of Eve

Retrieving The Healing Gift Of The
Sacred Feminine For The Human Family
Through Myth and Mysticism

Heather Mendel

BOOKS

Winchester, UK
Washington, USA

First published by O Books, 2009
O Books is an imprint of John Hunt Publishing Ltd., The Bothy, Deershot Lodge, Park Lane, Ropley,
Hants, SO24 0BE, UK
office1@o-books.net
www.o-books.net

For distributor details and how to order please visit the 'Ordering' section on our website.

Text copyright: Heather Mendel 2008

ISBN: 978 1 84694 246 4

A CIP catalogue record for this book is available from the British Library.

Design: Stuart Davies

Cover design: Heather Mendel

Printed in the UK by CPI Antony Rowe
Printed in the USA by Offset Paperback Mfrs, Inc

O Books operates a distinctive and ethical publishing philosophy in
all areas of our business, from our global network of authors to
production and worldwide distribution.

CONTENTS

Excerpts from the following titles are reprinted with kind permission of the author and/or publisher:

The River of Life: Spirituality, Judaism, and the Evolution of Consciousness by Rabbi Lawrence Kushner, ©1993, 1990 and 1981 Jewish Lights, Vermont, 1993

Standing Again at Sinai, ©1990 by Judith Plaskow, Harper Row, New York, 1990

The Heavens Declare: Astrological Age and the Evolution of Consciousness, by Alice O. Howell, ©1990, Quest Books, Illinois, 2006

Gates of Prayer: The New Union Prayerbook: adaptation from Ralph Waldo Emerson by Chaim Stern, Central Conference of American Rabbis. Copyright ©1975. Used by permission of Central Conference of American Rabbis. All rights reserved.

Chaim Stern in *Gates of Repentance: The New Union Prayerbook for the Days of Awe* Copyright © 1978 by Central Conference of American Rabbis from *Belief and Action, An Everyday Philosophy*, Adapted by Chaim Stern, by Viscount (Herbert Louis) Samuel (1870-1963), Pan Books, 1953, pp. 67f. Used by permission of Central Conference of American Rabbis. All rights reserved.

Myth and Reality in The Old Testament, by Brevard Childs with permission of SMC Press.

Unlocked Doors, by Danny Siegel, Town House Press, 1983

Acknowledgements:

To Susan Dressler, Beverly Engel, Susan Hoffman, Alice O. Howell, Pam Logan, Lisa Mendel-Hirsa, Eve Neuhaus, Cathy Pieters, Ethel Sosna and Simone Viola, my words of thanks are totally inadequate for the many hours of your precious time you devoted to this project. I appreciate your whole-hearted enthusiasm, suggestions, ideas, assistance and encouragement.

To Riane Eisler, thank you for lifting the veil, revealing my feminist journey ahead and to Judith Plaskow for challenging me to revisit and re-envisage the Jewish tradition in which I dwell and which dwells within me. I thank you for reminding me of the words of *Mishna Avot* (2.16): *It is not incumbent upon us to complete the task, but neither are we free to desist from it.* The final chapter of your book *Standing Again At Sinai* seeped softly into my soul as the impetus to my quest without my even being aware of it:

> "Creating new, diverse and egalitarian communities lead us to a new understanding of divinity, which in turn calls us to draw the circle of community ever wider . . . As we work towards the creation of a feminist Judaism as part of a larger struggle toward a more just world, we place our small piece in a mosaic that will finally provide a new pattern — a new religious and social order."
>
> *Kein y'hi ratzon*
> May this be Your will. Amen

My heartfelt thanks go to all of my teachers — my parents, children and grandchildren, the wonderful members of all classes and groups I have facilitated, all the inspiring authors (both those named in this book and those who are not) whose works have brought me hours of delight, lifting my spirit and deepening my understanding.

To Lisa, your Virgo proclivity for detail enhanced by your clarity of thought and innate curiosity have been honed by your legal training. Combined with a heart opened by compassion and joy, you were the caring editor for whom every writer longs and remain the daughter for whom every mother hopes.

To my husband Norm, in whose shelter I rest: Your generous, loving spirit, encouragement and commitment has shown me the possibility, potential and fulfillment of sacred partnership. I love you and am awed by all that you are.

Preface

Roots and Wings

There are two lasting bequests we can give our children: one is roots,
the other is wings.
Hodding Carter

Change is inevitable — however, I often wonder what Hannah would think. Hannah was my maternal great-grandmother whose Hebrew name I was given. Now, as a grandmother myself, I marvel at her resolve. Living in Eastern Europe at the time of the pogroms at the end of the nineteenth century, she had to accept the necessity of sending her children far away, facing the distinct possibility of never seeing them again. In our cyber-space era, with all the modern technological gadgets that shrink distances, it is almost impossible to imagine how such women felt. The potential and hope for better lives for their children — and the next generation — kept such families buoyant; the best she and the other women like her could hope for, would be contact with their children through the mail. The time span between sending and receiving such letters would be long enough to know that much would have changed in the interim.

That I come from a long line of strong women is readily believable. As I speak to Jewish friends, I hear similar tales of admirable foremothers who were able to exhibit great fortitude within a religious framework deemed patriarchal. Jewish women may have had their roles constricted and opportunities limited, but within this tradition there was never any sanction of cruelty to women — foot-binding, female circumcision or sanction for the husband's right to "discipline" his wife. By today's standards, proscribed roles restrict choices for personal fulfillment and

1

maturation. At the same time, in generalized and stereotypical reporting, Jewish women, it seems, have been treated respectfully by their men — fathers, husbands and sons. Conventional wisdom states that Jewish men make good husbands. Whether in their DNA, learned while imbibing their mother's milk or from watching their fathers, most develop an inherent appreciation of and respect for women.

My family stories focus around Hannah, a respected and much-loved matriarch, whose children all left Eastern Europe — some seeking refuge on American shores, others going to South Africa, all in search of a better, safer life. What would she think, I wonder, if she were to know that I, the great-grand-daughter named for her would leave South Africa, the country of my birth, for the same reasons?

Like the majority of those in the South African Jewish community, my grandparents came to South Africa from Riga at the close of the nineteenth century. I have been told that Hannah was a Torah scholar and people came from far distances for her counsel. I have no idea if it is true, but I love the story.

South Africa in the late 1890s was reeling with the discovery of gold and diamonds. It was a good time for entrepreneurial development. Arriving in the newly developing city of Johannesburg, Yiddish-speaking immigrants from Eastern Europe came with neither proficiency in the English language nor professions that could have eased the transition into their new lives. Like immigrants the world over, they settled in a strange and foreign land with hope in their hearts. Often arriving one family member at a time, they prayed for a better life than the one they knew, while at the same time, longing for the good things from the past they had left behind.

That generation passed on their Orthodox Jewish practice to their children. My parents described their early years as first-generation South Africans enjoying and being challenged by very different life experiences from anything their parents could have imagined. Like their contemporaries, they were raised in large families whose lives were rich in love if not in material possessions. Their reminiscences of loving family ties glossed over the ongoing family squabbles that inevitably plague families, especially immigrant families dealing with the stresses of living in a foreign land. The legacy of these arguments would continue between my mother and her siblings into their adult lives. Some disputes lasted for several years at a time. I grew up thinking that this was the way all families behaved. Over the years, the family *fahribbels* (squabbles in South African Yiddish) learned in my grandparents' generation were eventually forgotten in swirling reminiscences of the "good old days."

Unorthodox Beginnings

In Johannesburg in the early 1940s, my parents were older than most when they met and married. It was obviously a point of sensitivity for my mother, as she would never reveal her age. For as long I can remember, when asked how old she was she would reply with a coy smile, "I am twenty-nine and some months." Unlike my mother, I am happy to reveal my age to the world, but my weight remains a top secret. We all have our sensitivities.

My parents' courtship was brief. Just a few months after meeting, on a winter afternoon in August 1943 in a synagogue in Johannesburg, my parents stood excitedly under the *chuppah* (Hebrew for wedding canopy). As the rabbi began chanting the *brachot* (blessings), a stirring in the congregation interrupted the ceremony. My mother turned to see what distracted the rabbi and, to her horror, saw her beloved mother lying on the floor behind them. She had suffered a heart attack and died.

I cannot imagine how the ceremony proceeded, but it did. In recounting these events, my parents would tell me that in Judaism, life takes precedence over death. What was to have been the happiest day of my mother's life became an incomprehensible nightmare. The timing of these two major events in her life would haunt her for the rest of her days. The shock of this incongruous happenstance of joy and tragedy deeply affected both my parents. It started them on a spiritual search that went beyond the normal limits of questions posed by Jews regarding life after death, in turn affecting my early years.

During my childhood, dinner conversation in our home often included topics of rabbis and reincarnation, *kashrut* (kosher laws) and karma, the sacred and the secular, as my parents integrated their interests, religious and spiritual. It may have set into motion their next radical departure from tradition — radical at least, at that time. Early in their marriage, they decided the strictures of orthodoxy that had worked for their parents, were not the basis of a lifestyle they wanted for themselves. My parents were among the founding families who brought Reform Judaism to South Africa in 1947, a form of Judaism that stressed a concern for social justice and the welfare of all, so vital in the diabolically cruel and depraved system of *apartheid* (fittingly correctly pronounced as "apart-hate") that was becoming the law of the land.

As practicing Reform Jews, we learned to regard questions as more important than the answers they generated, an attitude that was to shape my spiritual life as an adult. We questioned the status quo of a South Africa in which we as Jews, members of the white privileged minority, were able to flourish at the expense of the oppressed indigenous peoples of the land. We had to find ways of living an ethical life in an immoral environment. This religious and spiritual atmosphere of my childhood provided fertile soil for the seeds of my own growing interest in the relationship between the physical and the spiritual that would be the impetus for my personal odyssey.

Exodus

Far more than merely a story in the Bible, exodus has been an aspect of the reality of Jewish life experience for thousands of years. Mystically and mythically, the first exodus was the separation of humanity from Divinity symbolized by Adam and Eve's departure from Eden. Our history continues with Abraham leaving Ur, Jacob traveling to Egypt, Moses to the Promised Land and after the destruction of the Second Temple, the Jewish people being scattered in what we have come to call the diaspora.

The forces of separation and movement from the old to the new take place on many more levels than just the physical. I feel certain Hannah would have understood my physical exodus from South Africa to America. I cannot but wonder what she would have made of the spiritual odyssey that would lead her great-grand-daughter to mysticism? Living mystically is a process, as contemporary as it is ancient, innovative and inter-pretative. Kabbalah, a source of the inner, mystical core of Judaism is emerging center-stage in the consciousness of many. Its hidden wisdom is being sought and revealed in ways never before imagined. Traditionally one had to be male, forty years of age and well-versed in Torah to study this mysterious body of wisdom. Today, peculiarly, thanks to several Hollywood stars, many of whom are not Jewish, more people than ever are curious about its teachings.

My introduction to kabbalah came in my early thirties and as each year passes, my understanding of mysticism broadens and deepens. The injunction for such study to start at forty suggests life experience will offer a more grounded understanding; however, for those fascinated with the unexplained, the subtle and the mysterious, mysticism may call at an earlier age.

What would Hannah have thought of a milieu in which it would be possible and meaningful not only for women like me to study the hidden, mystical approaches to our ancient faith but to be able to share these teachings with men and women of differing religious backgrounds? As the wise-woman I choose to imagine her to be, would she find my mystical passion more or less shocking than my feminist leaning? I assume she may have understood the desire for a spiritually meaningful life connecting me to something greater than myself. But feminism? Oh, that loaded word! How would she have reacted to the thinking of contemporary women who reject the patriarchal images, language and tone of the Judaism that Hannah presumably knew and practiced?

In my teens and early twenties, how could I have envisaged myself confronting my faith with eyes opened to a totally new way of seeing, forever changed by the questions of feminist scholars? How could I have foreseen that I would come to envisage Eve as humanity's quintessential unsung heroine? I clearly recall the moment of wonder when the veil (that I had not yet even realized clouded my vision) was drawn aside allowing me to glimpse a new and powerful possibility of the story of the development of humankind. Less than a year after I arrived in the United States in 1986, coincidently, I happened to see a television interview with Riane Eisler who had just published her book, *The Chalice and the Blade.* Coincidence, they say is God's way of remaining anonymous!

I knew nothing about the author and the subject she was discussing with the interviewer regarding the thesis of her book and the presentation she would be giving at Harvard that evening. I listened to her descriptions of a possible pre-patriarchal culture in the Ancient Near East, in which the Divine was worshipped as Goddess. The society she described was based on a partnership model between women and men rather than the hierarchical one in which we function. I was captivated by her words. Why had I never heard any of this before? Why, at a gut level did it feel so true?

I stood in the midst of the paradox — a moment that would inspire my lifelong quest. On the one hand, my intellectual self, schooled in the best that Western society had to offer was totally ignorant of what she was suggesting, while an intuitive awareness within hummed with a mysterious knowingness, previously concealed, now revealed. How to balance the two?

Which side to choose? History as it had been taught — or a previously unreported "herstory" intuited as valid, ancient and somehow inexplicably familiar?

I always felt that a personal relationship with Divinity was central to my life. God, I assumed without question, was male, for this was the way Divinity was imaged and labeled in both the Bible and prayer books to which I was exposed. In my forties, I awakened to the possibility of something different and more expansive. I found myself questioning the very nature of God — the Wholly One to whom I pray in the sanctuary of my own soul as well as the God I congregationally encounter as a Reform Jew.

How did my relationship with God affect my experiences on this human journey? Where was the hand of Divinity in all the coincidences that sparkled through my life? Was I, by the power of attraction, creating my own destiny by becoming aware of those serendipitous coincidences and synchronicities that I found and followed — or was I following a path foreseen, finding in the journey the hand of Divinity?

All my questioning seemed to narrow down to an under-standing of the nature of The Eternal and our relationship to that Source. Eve, it seemed, held the key. If she had been regarded as our most sacred heroine instead of being cast into the role of the ultimate villain in the history of the human family's sojourn on Earth, how would our lives be different?

The image of exodus and the symbol of the wandering Jew have thus been more than just physical in my family. From Lithuania to California by way of South Africa, from Orthodox Judaism to mysticism by way of Reform Judaism, and from patri-archy to egalitarianism by way of feminism. A multi-layered wandering indeed! The forces of separation and movement that cause us to leave behind the known and familiar and move into the unknown with hopes held high are aspects of human growth that apply to humanity. Are we, the Jewish people, on a metaphoric level, symbolic and stereotypical of that reality for the rest of the human family?

Separation and Movement

I now believe I was always headed on a search for the Sacred Feminine and her place, if any, in Judaism. In *apartheid* South Africa, I saw first-hand the tragically divisive nature of the patriarchal political system of "us and them" based on racial discrimination and reinforced by its practice. Not only was this system hatefully destructive towards those it considered subhuman because of the darker color of their skin, it was diabolical in allowing others to believe in their own racial superiority because of a pale complexion. As a child I started to become aware of the appalling effects of *apartheid* at the same time I was learning about the horrific results of Nazi racism directed against the Jews of Europe. My consciousness (and conscience) about discrimination were focused on racism — both as it applied to other Jews in far-off lands and as it applied so brutally all around me. Racism was so blatant that the less obvious sexist trends, hidden but nonetheless present and active, remained in the shadows of that extremely patriarchal society. After arriving in the United States and beginning to understand the concerns and anger of the feminist movement, I realized that racism and sexism stem from the same fear of difference.

Spurred on by Judith Plaskow's *Standing Again At Sinai*, I needed to look at my own tradition and ask some hard questions: Have the written texts of Judaism, the Bible and other sacred works so treasured in our community, been used in any way to foster the discriminatory systems that are part of a patriarchal mindset? How does belief in a monolithic male God affect both women and men? Do my feelings about Divinity that come through an intuitive knowing match my thoughts? Where in Judaism was the Great Goddess, widely worshipped in pre-patriarchal cultures all over the world? Who was Eve and what is her legacy?

Even though Jewish women may not have suffered as much as women who have lived under fundamentalist interpretations of traditions that demonstrate a punitive attitude towards women, what was there in Judaism that troubled the early Jewish feminists? And paradoxically, how is it that this patriarchal religion has birthed generations of strong, independent and assertive women — and men who love and respect them?

Dancing In The Footsteps of Eve is about change and becoming. It invites the reader to look at the names and labels we use for God. Do we create an image of God in our own likeness, describing our own values as we spiritually mature? Does our understanding of God have anything to do with the essence and attributes of The Ineffable Source of Life, or is it merely a reflection of ourselves? Influenced and shaped by feminism, mysticism and myth, this book came into being because of a deep egalitarian longing and a spirituality that moves us beyond the justifiable anger initially kindled in response to injustice. Through the kabbalistic concept of The Four Worlds, the book takes readers through the four levels of intuition, thought, emotion and action. These Four Worlds represent different and complementary levels of awareness that correspond to the mystical teaching of the stages in which The Holy One calls, creates, forms, and makes the world.

At the first level of Intuition the Sacred Feminine is seen and felt. She helps shape belief and self-worth. At the second level of Thought, in the "either/or" world of logic and reasoning the Sacred Feminine is concealed from view. She occasionally and briefly allows us to sense that She is still present and beckons to us to find Her. At the third level of Emotion, compassion, loving-kindness, and harmony are goals that that we strive for as we long for Her return. We sense Her presence although She remains mostly hidden. At the fourth level, Action, our expression of blessings (*brachot*) reminds us constantly of Divinity in our lives. We translate creed to deed (*mitzvot*) by living righteously. In this manner the Sacred Feminine can be re-imaged and reinstated in our interactions with one another. We continue to unfold, constantly opening layer upon layer of awareness. This evolution propels us towards sacred service that makes the world better because we are in it as we learn to replace our fear of difference with a celebration of diversity.

On the stages of our inner worlds, many characters function for whom we write the script, including the Mystic, the Student, the Dreamer, and the Humanitarian — all who draw sustenance from our experiences as spiritual beings on a human journey in search of enlightened awakening and maturity. We reflect on their constant interaction as they respond and challenge one another in our day-to-day experience.

Just as Miriam led the women in a celebratory dance at the shores of the Red Sea as they were about to realize their liberation from slavery, we can come together in celebration and dance on the shore of the Dead Sea of Patriarchy, timbrels held high. We will find our commonality with our sisters from other faith traditions. As we cross over to take our rightful places, the community will be enriched by the gifts we offer. In re-uniting women and men in a new way of honoring the otherness of each, we too can birth a new way of being.

Such thoughts do not easily fall into any recognizable category; for some Jews they may not seem Jewish enough, for some feminists, not feminist enough. I hope the following chapters will strike a chord with those whose spirit is catching the wave of the new paradigm as it ripples towards the shores of our present understanding, bringing with it a new way of being.

As a Jewish journey to spirituality, I use the word "Bible/Torah" sometimes referred to as The Old Testament. My dating system uses B.C.E (Before the Common Era) and C.E. (Common Era) instead of B.C. and A.D. I refer to the Ancient Near East as a distinct time and place in our history. A glossary can be found at the end of the book for unfamiliar words from languages other than English.

The inspiration for this journey comes, as inspiration often does for many Jews, from biblical text:

> "Get thee out of thy country and from thy kindred and from thy father's house unto the land that I will show you. And I will make of thee a great nation and bless thee . ." Genesis 12

The "father's house" that we are invited to leave is the patriarchal interpretation of Judaism, not its spiritual essence. We need to look back into our ancient past to recover what has been lost. We must retrieve what has been forgotten and bring it back to enrich our tradition for the totality of what it offers the present and the future. This incentive to re-imagine is attracting many more than just the Jewish community. Humanity is in the midst of leaving the "father's house," leaving behind what was believed to be factual in the patriarchal era and moving into an unknown future. We are uncomfortable with its unfamiliarity. It takes the courage of Eve to leave the known, armed only with faith. Discomfort can, however, bring unimaginable rewards, as our own life experiences demonstrate.

Our journey begins as we leave our "fathers' house," trusting in the Divine promise of blessing as we traverse new ground. We are re-enacting and revitalizing an ancient myth of exodus. Is this journey fictional? One person's fantasy is another's fact. My offering, a collection of stories and narrative, is a dance between the two. Where one begins and the other leaves off I invite your consideration. Join the dance, accompanying me as we uncover the eternal Sacred Feminine in Her many guises — The *Shechinah*, *Hochmah*, Hagia Sophia and all other names by which She makes Herself known.

In the beginning: a story

Come, come with me.
We must leave.
The house is starting to crumble.
Step outside.
Look, really look at the house.

It is very old. It has stood for some three thousand years. Its thick walls are bowed with age. See how it seems to have shifted on its base during the earthquakes. Now we can see that its foundation is not even. Look closer. Look down, far down, beneath its base. What is this? Another house? Older still, it seems to have been destroyed in order for this one to be built.

How strange that surviving in this house for all these years, we never knew, never even suspected, that it covered an older home. Step back from these two houses, one superimposed upon the other, and come with me. We must build a new house, a home, solid on the Earth that will provide security for our children, a house that can live with and respect the elements of Nature, in which we and our children will not only survive, but thrive. We will remember the house in which we lived. We will come to understand that mysterious house upon which it is built. In our new home, we will remember them both.

The house we are leaving is the house of our fathers. It is the interpretation of Divinity as they understood it. Built from the words they wrote on parchment, lovingly, by hand, with awe and wonder at the majesty of Divinity, they built this house of many rooms. Thick inner walls they built to divide us from each other. We never really grew up together as a family, sharing our talents for the benefit of all. The house of our fathers was never really secure, built as it was on an uneven foundation. We will take the texts from the library of this house. We will re-read and reinterpret them in our new home, and we will remember.

Now we have seen that under its crumbling walls are the remnants of the house on which they built. This was the house of our great-grandmothers. We did not even know that they had built a house. No. It was kept secret for a long, long time; but now the first house is revealed. The secret is out.

Our fathers' house was built to cover the home of our great-grandmothers. Instead of building a new house on the Earth, our fathers built over that ancient dwelling, covering it, they thought, forever. But they did not understand the nature of the Earth — her power, her storms and her quakes. She is revealing to us the secrets of the past.

Our great-grandmothers' house did not have inner walls to separate us. Living together was a shared and communal experience. There was time and place for privacy for all members of the family, as well as open space within the ancient home for all to share. This house had no library of written words. Our great-grandmothers were artists, not writers. They left us their art buried in the Earth from which it came: exquisite, hand-crafted clay treasures, molded as lovingly from the fullness of their hearts as the texts our fathers reverently scripted evolved from the considerations of their minds. Our great-grandmothers' legacy to us was made of the Earth. It came from the depths of being. They shaped the warm, living clay, slippery-soft solid silk, firmly in their hands. They strengthened it by flame and decorated its hardened surfaces with a painted language of symbols — not words, but a language nonetheless, telling of their lives, of their interpretation of Divinity.

From our great-grandmothers' house, too, we will take the treasures they left for us, to adorn and use in the new home that we will build. Books from our fathers, vessels and figurines from our great-grandmothers. We will remember them.

What is the earthquake that unsettles our fathers' house to reveal the secret of our great-grandmothers' house beneath? It is the ongoing rumblings of our own maturity, coming in waves, gentle swells that increase in velocity, then quiet for a while, the contractions of the Earth as she settles herself for the birthing of a new age. The wave that carries us buoyantly now is the wave of feminist scholarship, showing us how to look at our ancient world anew.

We now see that our fathers' house, an interpretation of reality describing our relationship to each other and to Divinity, was based on their written words that became our sacred texts. These words were composed some three thousand years ago and were taken from the oral tradition of our ancestors in the Ancient Near East. The oral tradition is very much older than the written one, and much more vast. The scribes involved in the writing of the text had to select the stories they considered important enough to be transcribed as a basis of what would become the law. They had to choose which version of each tale fitted their own perceptions of reality, for there were many versions from which to choose. Much was omitted, by chance or by design.

The oral tradition of our family probably filtered down to us via the almost forgotten civilization of Sumer in the fertile crescent between the Tigris and Euphrates rivers known as Mesopotamia — the region of modern Iraq. This is where history had its birth. There was life before history, however, as we keep discovering. Artifacts found throughout the world, dating back at least thirty thousand years, challenge the scribe's notion of the world being six thousand years old, as the Jewish calendar tells us. Our written history may be of that vintage; life and the world are far older.

Humanity's poetic storytellers — mystics and mythologists, magicians all — have described a mythic past of peace and tranquility, shimmering through the mists of time. Was this a dream? Or was it a collective human memory of our great-grandparents' garden to which we will now return as visitors? Is this the spiritual realm into which mysticism leads, a place beyond the borders of our minds, a place of awareness, an undiscovered space in consciousness for which we yearn? What is this mysterious dimension and how can we know it? Making use of all aspects of our being, our intuition as well as our intellect, our hopes and desires, we will attempt to reach what is but a faint memory burning deep within ourselves.

As we prepare for the journey, a few discomforting questions begin to surface. Are we returning to our great-grandmothers' house to stay? No, we will visit and become reacquainted. Our lives are fuller when we know who we are. By leaving our fathers' house, are we leaving God? No, we are leaving only an interpretation of Divinity that was built on uneven ground. By leaving our fathers' house, are we leaving our religious traditions? No, we are re-interpreting our past to encompass a greater reality than we were given.

Just as each generation has wanted to know, to unravel the mysteries of who we are, why we are here, and where we are going, we, too, want to know Divinity, to understand the Mystery. We want an answer to perhaps the greatest mystery of all — do we travel alone through time and space, on this journey called life? How do we come to understand Divinity — that limitless Source of All that Was, Is and Shall be?

Divinity is here, was there, and will always be. Each generation, women and men together, must rebuild the house. We left the old one standing too long, and that is why our fathers' house is now crumbling.

This journey to the mystery of our past will reveal the meaning of our myths. As archeo-mythologists, our tools for discovery will be the stories we will hear with our hearts; the artifacts we find, we will sense with our souls. This journey is a woman's spiritual voyage of discovery into the ancient realm of mythology.

What do we mean by egalitarianism, spirituality, mythology and Judaism?

Egalitarianism is an attitude of honoring The Other. Egalitarians will build the new house. "Patriarchists" built our fathers' house, dividing up the living space with many thick walls. Some rooms were large and enjoyed all the amenities and views to the outdoors; others were tiny, placed somewhere at the back of the house, as afterthoughts — windowless, and spartan. Men controlled the house and allotted the rooms. Women were assigned the tiny rooms at the back, furnished with beds on which to create and birth future generations. The cooking hearth too, was the women's domain. This was the way it was supposed to be, or so our fathers thought.

Egalitarians, like the feminists before them, knowing this social structure is wrong, are willing to tear down those walls of our fathers' house that separate and divide us. We celebrate diversity, honoring difference as sacred. In the house that we will build, no one will assign rooms by gender, color, or belief. All will be free to choose their own personal space.

Spirituality comes from the fire in the hearth at the center of the home. The fire is Life. The fire is Divinity. A spark of the fire dwells within each living being. The eternal sparks are the same; the fire is one. The human bodies in which the sparks reside are unique and temporal. We all look at the flames as we warm ourselves, and perhaps the fire looks different to each of us. Mystics interpret the signs for us all; kabbalists interpret from a Jewish perspective. Although the fire is one, our views may be different, depending on where we are seated and what our past experience with fire has been. Fire can warm. Fire can burn. Fire must be treated with respect and wonder. Spirituality is the light from the flames of life that warms our existence and connects us to each other, and the centrality of the fire that is Divinity.

Mythology refers to our interpretation of life's truths, too complex for us to understand in a simple and direct way. These are the stories, allegories, narratives, and tales we use to encompass and explain the inexplicable. Unlike the popular use of the word, here, "myth" does not refer to something untrue, but as author Jean Houston defines it, "something that never was and always is." Jung explained myth as stories for the psyche. Mythologists deal with patterns — archetypes of personalities and situations that live within our minds, offering us chances to play different roles on the stage of Life.

Judaism is a way of life as ancient as it is modern. It is the name for a covenant we have with Divinity. It is text based, evolving, mindful, and questioning. This-worldly, it is a family-based way of life that places its family members, born good, in a God-conscious, intimate relationship with Divinity. It understands freewill as a basic right and responsibility for all. In accepting this partnership, we agree to heal, restore, and transform the unfolding world in exchange for Divine blessing and guidance. The covenant is an ongoing commitment whose terms are constantly being revised and renewed. For this reason, Judaism remains a way of life that is modern. The covenant is as timely as it is timeless. Reform Judaism's embrace is wide and inclusive and encourages growth and fulfillment for all.

Come then, we are ready to begin. With our stories and our figurines, we are prepared for this egalitarian journey into the spirituality of our past. Come, come with me.

Part One: Intuition

The Sacred Feminine Revealed

Truth is one and the people call it by different names.
From the Rig Veda

Father Time on Mother Earth

What do we know of the world before the beginnings of Judaism? It seems important to look at the then-known world and its belief systems as we try to understand the sweep of time through history.

The story of Creation and that of Adam and Eve in the Garden of Eden comprise the Jewish myth of our genesis. Other faith traditions have developed their own tales about humanity's beginnings on Earth. All these stories are just that — stories or allegories attempting to answer our most basic questions about our origins and destiny. All these tales are ancient, their sources lost in the mists of time.

In the last decades of the twentieth century we sent technologically advanced craft from Earth into the cosmos, increasing our understanding of the furthermost limits of space. Photographs from the Hubble space telescope leave us breathless, in awe of the splendor and mystery of the Universe. Concurrently, we are expanding our awareness of times past by discoveries on the face of the Earth and under her oceans, as we try to piece together the mystery of our beginnings.

It is difficult to comprehend the forces that shaped preceding civilizations so different from our own, even with concrete evidence of their lifestyle and values. These mysteries are part of what make the idea of time travel so appealing. We love to imagine ourselves in Renaissance Italy, biblical Israel, or Ancient Egypt, cultures hundreds or thousands of years distant from us. What then of bygone eras, removed from us by many more thousands of years?

Who built Mohenjo Daro in India, the Sphinx in Egypt, or Çatal Huyuk in Turkey? Who sculpted the statues of Easter Island? Hints of the existence of civilizations about which we previously knew nothing, are being revealed to us. Scholarship, and particularly feminist scholarship — in the areas of history, anthropology, and archeo-mythology is helping us piece together the fragments of our origins, drawing us back into the uncertainty of prehistoric mystery.

Time, that master of order in the world of history, has no power in the realm of the amorphous collective memory, where as our prayer books tell us, "a thousand years are like yesterday." *Chronos* and *Kairos* are two archetypal markers of time — *Chronos* horizontal and superficial, *Kairos* vertical, leading into the depths. *Chronos* is that logical, mighty, masculine keeper of clocks and calendar, of past and future, while *Kairos* is a portal to the eternal now, the present, and can be likened to the intuitive swirling, feminine space of "once-upon-a-time." Like dancers on the stage of eternity, these two aspects of time are locked in an eternal tango in which the ever-present *Chronos* sets the rhythm and beat for an unfolding reality. *Kairos* confounds us with the color and flow of movement which tantalize us with a sense of new possibilities — ancient tales from the world of myth and story that reveal and then conceal themselves once more.

As *Kairos* dips and swirls into awareness, we grasp for the ephemeral filaments of an alternate and complementary reality that seems to withdraw just as we reach out. *Kairos* introduces chaotic sparks of possibilities that slip in and out of the pattern of order established by *Chronos*. *Kairos* is a portal to an eternal, imaginative dimension that is home to our souls; the realm's "lingua franca" of imagery is its language.

Our history swirls around in our thoughts as a chaotic mass of telescoped events, as chains of cause-and-effect phenomena that somehow lose their sequential connections. We confuse the impact of events that may have happened thousands of years ago with those of a million years before. The first book of the Bible, when read literally, does not help. It describes the creation of the Universe in six days. Literally read, six twenty-four hour periods, which led to the belief, still held curiously by some, that the world is a few thousand years old. Such readers miss the point that this story is sheer poetry speaking to the soul in the metaphor that it understands.

We have historical evidence of the civilization that existed in Egypt thousands of years ago. Dwelling in *Chronos*, we assume the people we read about in our history books and know through their papyrus scrolls and carved hieroglyphics, were responsible for all the ancient monuments in and around the area of the Nile. By compressing time, we skip the possibility that the Great Pyramid and/or the Sphinx, as suggested by writer John West and geologist Robert Schoch, may have existed as ancient monuments before the development of the Egyptian culture we have come to know through its artifacts and hieroglyphs.

In *Kairos*, the vastness of space and time eludes our understanding. Outdoors, in contact with Nature, we sense its profundity most clearly. For sophisticated city dwellers, a visit to the stillness of the Grand Canyon or Yosemite, the ocean viewed from a precipitous cliff, or a few moments of meditation under a giant Californian redwood, allows us the opportunity to sense immensity. Standing silently, open and vulnerable to the grandeur and age of Nature, we feel humbled at our puny size and at the same time, elated at being a small part of this huge miracle. There is a Jewish adage that suggests we keep two notes in our pockets at all times, the first reminding us: "For my sake was the universe created," while the second adds, "I am but dust and ashes."

In the grandeur of the natural world, few can help but listen to the silence. In that stillness, we hear the wordless songs of the Earth. Rocks and wind combine to sing, their song audible to us when we still the busyness of our urban lives long enough to listen. People who live close to the Earth hear the sounds and know the songs. Their lives move with the natural rhythm of the dance.

In such settings, we are forced to question the dating of the world according to the Jewish calendar as a mere seven thousand years. Presently, science seems to accept the age of the universe to

be more than thirteen billion years. Our solar system is specu-
lated to be some four and a half billion years old and our planet
Earth, a latecomer to the celestial party, a mere four billion years.
Science informs us that mammals were created two hundred and
fifty million years ago, and the extinction of the dinosaurs
occurred sixty-five million years ago. I am no mathematician —
when math genes were being doled out, it seems I was at the
back of the line. However, even I can understand something of
the immensity of this time line of four billion, to two hundred
million, and then sixty-five million years ago. According to the
Genesis account of creation then, each biblical "day" must have
lasted many millions of years. How can we read this story as
anything but metaphor?

And what of human beings? Anthropologists, paleontolo-
gists, and archeologists were baffled with some footprints
discovered in volcanic ash in Tanzania that looked remarkably
human. The problem for science is that these footprints date back
three and a half million years! It appears that around five million
years ago, the climate in the Rift Valley in Central Africa
changed, due to movements in the Earth's crust, and it is
probable that early hominids moved from the treetops to the
ground. Scientists working with DNA, and mitochondrial
evidence in particular, suggest that we all have a common ances-
tress known as the African Eve. The theory is controversial but
acknowledged as an important contribution to the study of our
human origins. Brian Swimme, author of *The Hidden Heart Of The
Cosmos* suggests that from our present understanding, human
culture dates back some two hundred thousand years.

If we do not want to compress time, we can acknowledge that
eons passed before we had evidence of our earliest human-like
ancestors, the Neanderthals, some hundred thousand years, and
the Cro-Magnons, thirty thousand years ago. What is waiting
still to be discovered and dated beneath the sands of the Gobi
Desert or at the bottom of the Atlantic Ocean?

According to biblical scholars, Sarah and Abraham lived somewhere between 1800 and 1500 BCE, a mere thirty-five hundred years ago. What do we know of all those intervening millennia from three million to three thousand years ago? When did the Garden of Eden exist, if at all? Who was Eve? Adam? When did they live? And where was this fabled Garden? How do we travel back through time to understand prehistory as a sequence of events?

Measurement of time is a human device to help us understand reality. When we stand in awe at the magnificence of the natural world, we know that mountains, rivers, sky and clouds, winds and storms neither obey nor heed any clock or calendar. Mountains age, but in increments that cannot be sensed or measured by human perception within the span of a lifetime. How then to try to date the beginning of our creation? From a Jewish perspective, this is not of great significance. Being a "this world" religion our focus is more on how we live the life we have rather than concern ourselves with what came before or what will follow.

The Bible is the source of our belief regarding the creation. Each word, each sentence has multiple possibilities of meaning. The first Hebrew word in the Bible, *Bereishit*, can mean "in the beginning," "with beginningness," "with wisdom," or even "once upon a time." This compendium of sacred texts tells the ancient story of the creation of humankind from a Jewish perspective, dating back long before there were Jews. Adam, Noah and the generations before Abraham were not Jewish — these stories have a universal thrust that applies to all humanity. Adam, from the Hebrew word, *adamah*, meaning of the Earth, refers to all human beings (earthlings) born of the Earth and breathed to life by God. Jewish legend tells us we were created of red, yellow, black and white dust from the four corners of the Earth, reminding us of our similitude and equality.

These stories were told orally for eons before they were

24

written in their present form. Our challenge is to interpret and synthesize the many possible layers of meaning in the text. In our Temples, we do this with ongoing weekly study and find it amazing how the same words reveal themselves differently to us each year as we mature and see nuances and possibilities, now revealed, that seemed not to have been there previously.

The story of the Jewish people emerges from that of humanity, as a people in covenant with the Divine whose goal is to manifest Divinity on Earth; for this, they will be blessed. We understand our lives as an opportunity to express godliness in all we do, and to share this sentiment of holiness with all those we meet. In taking on this partnership for blessing, we accept the challenge of *tikkun olam* — reparation of the unfolding world that we, as co-creators in partnership with Divinity, are meant to heal and complete. The world in which we find ourselves is part of The Great Oneness, and our relationship to Nature should be one of reverential stewardship.

Judaism looks to the Torah to find the story of our beginnings. From the first few sentences of our creation story we intuit certain general assumptions about Judaism. Here, the language of the Bible is poetry rather than prose. In grandly eloquent imagery we see the unfolding of the creation that brings order from chaos. The Creator is limitless and infinite and sees everything that is created as good, including human beings who are created the image of the Divine.

Judaism teaches us that God is One, invisible and indivisible. God is good and we, as part of the Oneness of God, were born good and are here to manifest God's goodness on the Earth. God is both immanent and transcendent.

There is an interesting relationship of separation in the epochs of creation in the first few lines of the Bible. Days one and four deal with light from darkness, days two and five with air from water, days three and six with water from Earth and on day seven all is blessed and sanctified. The ancient elements of air, water, fire and earth are reflected in the story.

Judaism begins with faith. Our creation story describes in the inspiring voice of the poet, a creative God bringing balance into an inchoate void, and separating light from dark, land from water — creating conditions that would evolve to be conducive to life on the Earth, including human life. Created last, we have yet to learn with humility our role in the whole design that comprises each individual puzzle piece of life.

As no human was there to observe the creation, with faith we accept that a creative God brought this into being and that it was good. As each epoch, (in biblical terms, each day passed) God reviews what has been formed and says it is good. After the creation of human beings, God's poetic words reveal that we are born "very good" with a unique role to be in partnership with Divinity. From a Jewish perspective this means no original sin, no need for baptism. All is created "good."

In the image of God, we honor the creative ability we have been given. God is one, invisible, and indivisible. This Oneness comprises more than the monotheistic idea of one God. It is a constant reminder of the Oneness of Creator and creation, comprising everything and no-thingness, without boundaries or limits. In this infinity, human beings, finite, temporary and with limited free will, become part of the creation story with important roles to play. Although literalists count back the generations of biblical characters and come up with the date of almost six thousand years ago for the creation, few Jews consider the universe to be that young, understanding the poetry and metaphor of biblical language in the refrain "it was evening, it was morning, day one," and on through day seven—metaphors for epochs rather than seven twenty-four hour periods.

Biblical scholars count the generations mentioned in the Bible as dating back some 5700 years at the time of this writing, giving literalists the understanding that the creation occurred 5768 years ago. Unlike Christianity, Islam or Buddhism, Judaism does not center on the life and teaching of a savior. Ours is the story of the birth of the world, and offers a history of one group of individuals whose journey, individually and collectively, teaches universal, archetypal liberation and redemption. The amazing text we treasure is expansive enough to allow us to decide for ourselves what we choose to read as factual and what is metaphor. At the same time, it is deep enough for us shift through various layers and reflections of time, appreciating the gifts that both *Chronos* and *Kairos* bring.

In Search of the Intangible Garden

So, where do we come from? The Mystic within intuits many approaches to discovering our hidden past, ranging from the scientific to the mythical and mystical. We can use the skills and knowledge of scientists as they glean and interpret our past, acknowledging scientific research as just one avenue of discovery. The interpretation of archeological discoveries provides a rich field; so does the storytelling of ancient myths and legends — all pathways to learning about our past as a human family. As we listen to these ancient tales, we encounter fact, fantasy and faith. It is not easy to see where one begins and another ends.

Because we have no written or iconic history to prove our prehistoric development, anthropologists and archeologists dip into the realm of *Kairos*. From my childhood, I pictured our earliest beginnings in caves, such as those at Lascaux in France, or more particularly as a South African, the caves at Sterkfontien with which I was more familiar and where, in 1936, early hominid remains were discovered by Dr. Robert Broom.

The images with which we are familiar of that time span suggested a lifestyle as interpreted by male scholars who presumed life as we know it today must have similarly existed in prehistoric times. We are all familiar with the cartoons of club-bearing, pelt-clad "Flintstone" males, dragging their mates around by their flowing tresses. Really? What do we know about how these ancient beings viewed themselves? How did they relate to one another? How did they understand the ultimate mysteries of birth, life and death? Did they imagine Divinity in any way?

"Ontogeny recapitulates phylogeny" is a scientific theory that states the development of the child from conception to maturity is the same model on which humanity as a species evolves. It is a controversial theory. Jungian scholar and astrologer Alice O. Howell, suggests in her book *The Heavens Declare: Astrological Age and the Evolution of Consciousness* that just as the newborn child senses itself to be part of the mother's world, it is probable a group mentality rather than an individual sense of identity may have existed in our earliest beginnings.

Burials from the time of our cave-dwelling ancestors date back one hundred thousand years. The deceased were placed in fetal positions, covered with red ochre possibly reminiscent of the blood covering us at birth, which indicated an awareness of human rebirth in a world unseen, when the individual transitioned at death in "the womb and tomb" of Mother Earth.

Scientists tell us that over time, and with climatic changes, our ancestors came down from the caves, changing their life-style from hunter-gatherers to agrarian farmers and herders. The role of women in the hunter-gatherer communities was probably significant, considering that the staple of early humanity's food was most likely nuts, fruits, berries, and readily available greenery, while the protein they obtained from the hunt was more of a luxury than commonplace daily nourishment. Women's role in agrarian societies was, and is, important too. Caring for the family requires the ability to nurture both infants and the elderly, and to tend to plants gathered and finally grown for food and medications — and who better equipped for the job than women blessed with maternal instinct?

In his book *The Alphabet Versus the Goddess*, Leonard Shlain gives a comprehensive account of our earliest beginnings with an emphasis on the development of speech and language that differentiated us as a species. Gestures, he reminds us, were probably the earliest forms of communication, and may be the reason the palms of our hands are very pale, irrespective of the color of our skin, allowing gestures to be visible even with the loss of daylight.

The amazing advent of language allowed the evolving human family a method of sharing their constant amazement, delight, and fascination with their world and their increasing experience of the novelty of life. Swimme suggests that human development, as part of the constantly evolving process of which we are part, allowed us to extend our period of play as a species, giving us access to wonder, curiosity and freedom, as we help move forward the story of our expanding complexity.

With gestures came babble, the earliest of speech sounds which eventually evolved into language, overcoming the need for a complex gesture system. Ultimately, written language — symbols of symbols — became the overriding means of viewing our world and our lives, diminishing the importance of the image as symbol. Today when we visit art museums, Schlain asks how much time do we spend looking at the art form itself — painting or sculpture — as compared to the amount of time we take to read the information accompanying it? We rely heavily on language to inform us.

It is interesting to watch how speech and language develops in a newborn child. Bathed in sounds, the earliest communication stemming from the infant, other than crying, is the emotional facial gesture of a smile. Babble sounds are made for fun and reinforced as they approximate the words used in the language of the home. By the end of the first year of life, a vocabulary of single spoken words usually begins to form. Hearing babies are now being taught sign language allowing communication before the development of verbal language. This has helped to alleviate the earliest frustration of the infant in making its needs known.

Advances in science and medicine often follow on what already is understood by humanity's storytellers, artists, and poets. Many are the inventions that were sparked from a dream. Elias Howe was able to develop the sewing machine after dreaming of a needle with a hole at its point instead of its top. Chemist Friedrich Kekule was able to understand the structure of the benzene ring after dreaming of the snake swallowing its own tail. Dreams may originate in the same imaginal realm of *Kairos* as stories and myths, accessed through the functioning of the right lobe of the brain.

Neuroscientists explain that the different hemispheres of the brain not only handle different aspects of our experience, but that in utero, the right lobe of the brain develops first. According to Schlain, the grounding of our abilities to emote and to feel, to appreciate the rhythms of music or speech, and to recognize images in an "all-at-once" manner occurs before the development of the functions of the left lobe of the brain, where most of the language centers for both speech and reading are found and which function in linear "one-at-a-time" fashion.

The right-brained approach to reality may be the older and a more natural way of interacting with the environment and entering *Kairos*. Mythologists and mystics rely on right-brained access to information about reality. Their understanding about ourselves and our world comes through neither artifacts nor physiological/neurological studies of humanity; rather, they focus on the stories told of heroes and heroines, gods and goddesses. Ancient wisdom is accessible in this way too. It is fascinating to see the similarities in beliefs of different cultures and faith communities. Inner teachings, often hidden in myth and allegory, tell of the same universal laws at work, often veiled and disguised beneath layers of dogma, creed and ritual that we see in the outer world.

The words and images of the teachings may differ according to the experiences of the group to whom they are offered. The significance and symbolic power of the buffalo is comprehensible to indigenous Native Americans because of their experience and reverence for the herds that provided for them; in other physical locations these truths are worded and imaged differently to coalesce with the outer reality of the lives of the people being taught. Kabbalists, students of Jewish knowledge and mystical experience, describe the journey from the unconscious state to awareness in terms of light, the garden, and the Tree.

Simply told, a kabbalistic understanding starts with a belief that The Divine brought forth the Creation because The Divine wished to behold Itself. So intending, the Divine Creative Source of All That Is, Was and Shall Be, withdrew or contracted a space within Itself and into which the *Ayin Sof Or*, the Divine Beam of Light entered the chaotic, dark void and unfolded in ten stages, successive and simultaneous, that we image as the Tree of Life, allowing us to think about the attributes of Divinity, the destiny of humankind, and the nature of the universe. Told as a story, we are given the images of light within the first words of our teachings, and humanity's beginning is placed in a Garden at the center of which symbolically stand two trees as a sign of the duality that is the essence of life in the physical realm.

Creation stories form the foundation of the spiritual lives for those to whom the tales are told, in the words, symbols, and images that are meaningful in time and place for the listeners. From these differing experiences and understandings, rituals develop as outer expressions of the inner truth. Ritual, like language, is also symbolic — an outer garment of an inner living truth that can be used to separate us from one another instead of emphasizing the inner commonalities we share.

Mythologists and mystics are entranced by the images of the inner world. They study the imaginative stories, creative arts, and belief systems that form cultural underpinnings and tell of the inner life of the human family during their physical sojourn on Earth. Their vocabulary describes the realm unseen in terms of archetypes. Howell, in her book *The Heavens Declare* suggests the possibility that the precession of equinoxes, familiar to astrologers, may more deeply impact our mythic lives than we realize.

As she traces human development from ten thousand years ago, she demonstrates how "coincidently" during the two thousand years the Age of Cancer (whose glyph, thought of as a crab, can also be seen as the breasts of a woman) we have evidence of an epoch in human development in which Divinity is worshipped as the Great Goddess. As the next Age of Gemini (The Twins) settles, communication becomes integral. We have the first stories of a named male hero, Gilgamesh, and his despair at the death of Enkidu — his alter ego/ friend/ human counterpart? Our biblical history possibly reminds us of the ancient theme in the relationship between Cain and Abel.

As a new Age takes precedence, old images and symbols need to make way for the new. We find in the legends of many different cultures the young male hero slaying the ancient Mother. With the Age of Taurus, the symbol of the bull strongly predominates in the art of the ancient Minoans and in prehistoric Turkey. With the Age of Aries, in which Judaism is born, the Ram becomes a symbol for the era. It is fascinating to consider its symbolic role played in the mythology of our ancestors — the ram in the thicket is sacrificed instead of Isaac, the sheep's blood is used by the Israelites to mark their doors on the night of the last of the ten plagues so that the Angel of Death will pass over. The *shofar* — a ram's horn — is still used today to call us to awaken, to become conscious. Intriguing too, that when the Israelites revert to former worship practices at the foot of Mount Sinai, the object of worship is the Golden calf — the image and symbol from the previous era.

Myths, with their images concealed and disguised, beckon to

us. Although they are not tangible to our five senses, they are real, existing and exerting a powerful influence within the inner depths of our being. Mythic images direct the way in which we perceive reality and structure our lives and relationships. This is the place of dreams and imaginings, an inner stage that gives us the opportunity to play certain roles for a time until we have learned the lessons that our souls may require. Rabbi Michael Lerner, in his book *Jewish Renewal*, echoes a similar thought when he suggests that the receiving of the Ten Commandments is happening continuously, as each of us approaches "Mount Sinai" in our own psyches. As we grow silent and listen, we hear.

To the mythologist then, Nirvana, Mt. Olympus, or the Garden may simply be different names we associate with the symbolic image of that mystical and mythic place "that was, is and shall be." Such names are devised in *Chronos* while the images they attempt to define arises from *Kairos,* a time-and-space beyond the world we know. Mystics explain that this is a place of wholeness and completion from which we venture to experience life in a physical body, or in a "garment of skin" as we are told in the biblical tale.

Mythology is a bridge between the visible and invisible worlds. Its study opens an understanding of how groups of individuals view themselves and their gods, postulating that we create gods in the image of ourselves rather than the other way round. Cooperative creative communities from prehistory seemed to have worshipped Divinity as Goddess, the Sacred Feminine whose focus is life. The horse-mounted, arms-bearing warriors of the historical period, image Divinity as a warrior King who honors death.

The quest of both the mythologist and the mystic is to guide us inwards, away from our everyday experience and down towards our own depths, the unknown realm of images, dreams, and symbols. Crossing the Greek mythological "River Styx" is mysterious and can be scary. These depths are the place of The

Shadow, the unconscious realm of our lives that connects us to the larger collective unconscious. The purpose of studying mysticism is to come to know by inspiration, intuition, and reflection how to awaken to all of life's wonder. We learn how to make conscious those things that have slept in the depths for so long, the unloved, unwanted parts of ourselves that we relegate to The Shadow. Once we are conscious of experiences we shelved because we found them so disturbing, they no longer cause us fear. Here too, lies the potential for individual greatness, our spiritual evolution and maturity. From this same source, we become conscious of the creative powers we can utilize to transform the world and ourselves by grounding Divinity.

Outside the realm of scientifically verifiable pursuits is the insight of these mystics and mythologists. From them we learn that we are not limited by the borders of our physicality. We float in an ocean of spiritual energy and our individual beings are but droplets of that oceanic flow. Ah! but what droplets! Where does each drop begin and the ocean end? Harboring a spark of Divine consciousness within, we scatter and splash within the wave-crest. The winds lift us up from the undulations of the rolling waters and we fly, alone but part of the Grand Whole, experiencing this magical world as we learn to taste, touch, feel, see, and hear all that it has to offer.

All that can be gleaned about our prehistoric past is supposition — possible pasts for which we have little proof. Therein lies the mystery, confounding, confusing, and beckoning. Zechariah Sitchin, whose book *Genesis Revisited*, based his ideas on an interpretation of ancient Sumerian literature. He predicted some of what NASA's space probes would later confirm about the solar system. There are many interesting theories about the sudden leap forward in our evolution that occurred around ten thousand years ago. Suddenly we became literate after tens of thousands of years of an illiterate but creative human past. Why? As we read the different explanations, we can intuit what feels most authentic for ourselves.

Our Great-Grandmothers' House

As we move forward on the time line, we explore the eras in prehistoric times that have left some evidence of the peoples who preceded us. Just as the astronauts were taking giant forward leaps of faith and stepping onto the moon, our understanding of time relating to our beginnings has catapulted us farther back than we imagined possible. We are now asked to consider multiple possible pasts, rather than just accept the one version of history written by the patriarchal victors.

As women enter various fields of scholarship, they consider so-called "obvious truths" anew. We ask new and different questions because our perspective is different. This applies not just to the way we view the world, it applies to our very physicality. The medical profession has recently realized that the male medical model of wellness, once considered applicable to everyone, does not apply to women. As contemporary women and men we should re-evaluate what history teaches. Does the idea of history beginning six thousand years ago have any validity? Only to proponents of "creative intelligence." Such literalists choose to ignore the mounting evidence of thousands of years of human development before the advent of writing.

On a trip to Barcelona a few years ago, my attention was riveted on a banner flying high above the streets of the city. I saw the word "*Diosas*" as part of the text I could not read because my Spanish is poor; however that word, together with the readily understood image of the tiny carved figurine on the banner, left no doubt that the public was invited to view an exhibition of some ancient goddess figurines from around the globe.

The first such carving I had ever seen was a Cycladic goddess in a small New England museum. Its simple beauty was profound. I retain a clear memory of the white, five-inch marble figure, triangular head, arms folded over budding breasts, vulva finely engraved between the simplified legs. It was one of those serendipitous meetings between the figurine and I that "coincidently" happened at the same time I was reading *The Chalice and the Blade*. That tiny, white, carved figure served as a portal to my burgeoning awareness of the reality of our pre-historic past described by Eisler.

Almost twenty years later, I found myself serendipitously in Barcelona outside the Cultural Museum that was exhibiting a collection of ancient goddess figurines. I knew exactly what I wanted to see on that sunny summer morning in overcrowded Barcelona, teeming with tourists, streets jammed with tour buses. Descending down into the dark subterranean passages (I love the metaphor) I walked through the diggings of Old Barcelona that lie beneath the city and warmly responded to the sight of the old synagogue, its Hebrew letters still legible. The end of the walking tour led visitors further back in time through tunnels, to the gallery of the goddesses. I stood in awe seeing those exquisite female carvings — some just a couple of inches in height. These figurines had been discovered throughout Old Europe and the Ancient Near East. Some of the oldest dated back more than thirty thousand years.

On a conventional European visit, Americans marvel at buildings constructed eight hundred years ago. How do we comprehend the thousands of years that intervene between the time the figurines were created and the start of recorded history some ten thousand years ago? How many years of human development must have occurred prior to the carving of the Venus of Willendorf, a five-inch female statue found in Austria in the early twentieth century? From the work of archeologists we know that it takes time for groups of people to be able to create items of beauty. We also know that such people must have time for leisure, set aside from the daily needs of gathering and preparing food, clothing and shelter to devote to artistry. And for me, the most exciting and challenging aspect of all is trying to ascertain what was in the minds and hearts of these ancient artists that inspired the creation of these exquisite and reverential carvings?

Marija Gimbutas, former Professor Emeritus of Archeomythology at UCLA, in her book *The Language of the Goddess*, introduces us to the ancient figurines and other artifacts that she catalogued. Using her skills as an archeologist, linguist and mythologist, she brought the neolitihic and bronze cultures of "Old Europe" to public attention. Her work covers vast periods of time and space and encourages us to break through old notions of early human society. As a feminist scholar and theoretician, her findings have influenced many women scholars, including Riane Eisler. As a child, Eisler escaped from Nazi Europe where she witnessed the ultimate destructiveness of the patriarchal hierarchy, motivating her to ask if there was not another way that people could relate to one another, especially people from different backgrounds and perspectives. Through her intellectual scholarship and creative reasoning she suggests the possibility of the partnership model that may have been the basis of the early neolithic communities; these were not only goddess-centered, but creative, egalitarian communities of women and men who lived in beautiful surroundings. The remnants of their lifestyle showed villages built on valley floors rather than on mountain-tops, with evidence of neither walls for protection, nor signs of warfare and weaponry. Additionally there seemed to be an absence of class hierarchies based on gender. What was found in great abundance were the hundreds of "goddess" figures.

Just as women birthed new human beings from their bodies, it is easy to understand the assumption that the world was birthed by the Great Goddess. Neolithic graves and artifacts from Asia Minor and Old Europe indicate the important position of women in the community. They were seen as symbolic representatives of the Sacred Feminine on Earth. Their roles were consequently elevated and sanctified. The image of Divinity in female form may represent the earliest evidence we have that we create Divinity in our own image.

Is it a stretch to consider that the way we understand Divinity is a reflection of the way we see ourselves? That we create the image of Divinity in our own image? If we accept that there is a God, something beyond ourselves that we do not understand but sense, we will need to image and name the Mystery in some way. Creative, nurturing communities may worship a nurturing, creative Goddess, while warring, hierarchical societies that honor domination and the control of others may describe their God in similar terms.

We project our own image onto The Wholly One. Whether we see God as female or male does nothing to change the "beingness" of Divinity; the labels we select, however, do reflect our own spiritual evolution.

God. Goddess. Surely the names we use cannot affect the essence or nature of Divinity? We read the written words in front of us; the ancient oral storyteller is removed from the equation. The left-brain becomes the dominant interpreter of fact; with its speech and language centers, it is responsible for linear thinking — sequencing, the ability to abstract, and be logical. The right hemisphere, realm of the essential non-verbal clues on which we used to rely — the world of emotions, music, meditation, gesticulation, and spontaneity were superseded by the functions of the left brain. Mythology reveals an archetypal overthrow of the ancient Great Goddess by a young male God just as the left hemisphere of the brain became dominant in human development. The functions of the left hemisphere have come to be valued as our only valid means of processing experience.

Forbidden Fruit

Several years ago, in a local supermarket, a toddler listened to a woman's voice calling for an extra cashier at the registers. The child looked up to where the voice seemed to be emanating, and with eyes wide in amazement said: "That must be God's wife!"

God's wife! Hopefully within our lifetime, another child will say, with equal amazement and conviction, "That must be God!" Our conditioning starts very early, as does our sense of relationship with Divinity. My grandson's first God question came before he was two. Standing and looking at the rain that was preventing him from going out to play, I suggested we should say "Thank you dear God for the rain that makes the flowers grow." He turned to look at me and asked: "God? What's she's name?"

I remember too a story told by a woman rabbi. While out with her three-year old daughter, she met a male colleague. Introducing her daughter to him, the mother said: "I want you to meet Rabbi David." Incredulous, the child looked up at her mother and said: "Don't be silly, he can't be a rabbi. He's a man!" Conditioning may start early but norms change rapidly too!

Individually as well as communally, in a world as mysterious as it is beautiful, we start early to question our relationship to God and what connects us to a reality beyond the physical. We are fascinated with our origins and destiny and those great mysteries of birth and death around which all faith communities create rituals to mark these signal events. We are encouraged to ask questions.

Possibly because of the stress on the importance of study, questions seem to be an integral part of being Jewish. There is the old story about two Jews meeting and one asks the other: "How are you?" Shrugging his shoulders, the other responds, "How should I be under the circumstances?" Judaism has survived in part, I believe, because it has encouraged both humor and a questioning attitude to expand our boundaries — physical, emotional or intellectual. We include within our ranks a wide range of believers — from skeptical agnostics to self-assured fundamentalists. Liberal Jews are encouraged to question all aspects of our lives.

As a child, I was puzzled by an incongruity I discovered, although at the time I would not have known such a word. I marveled at the beauty of the illustrated Bible stories that I loved. Eve and the Garden of Eden particularly fascinated me — probably the inspiration for writing this book. As the first woman, she was, at least in my storybooks, golden-haired and delicate — a "Barbie doll" stereotype of femininity. When I first saw illustrations of Neanderthal and Cro-Magnon beings, I could not imagine how our human mother, Eve, had first given birth to these cave dwellers before us. They resembled her far less than we did. The artistic interpretation of the illustrator came, I naively assumed, from the possession of some magical knowledge to which I was not privy. I happily accepted it as factual. Puzzling to me as a child too, as described in the book of Genesis, Eve, Adam, and the serpent were poetically verbal, unlike our Neanderthal or Cro-Magnon ancestors. Did we as a species regress rather than progress?

I was still too young to realize that a literal reading of the texts was not going to suffice in my search for Divinity! In the egocentricity of my childhood, I was also too young to know that the Garden of Eden fascinated many more than just me. When we, as adults, think of the creation of humankind, how many Westerners immediately see, with the mind's eye, the painting in the Sistine Chapel of the finger of God reaching towards Adam? Is it collective memory that holds the picture of a magical garden in which we once lived? Is Paradise physical or spiritual? Did it once exist on Earth? As I got older, I realized this cherished mystery is more than just a Jewish memory. Around the world, on every continent, there are many cultures and civilizations that remember and long for the enfolding safety of the Garden.

Other questions that tantalized me (possibly related in more ways than I realized) revolved around what exists beyond the world of our five senses. Are there more colors than we can see?

What would they look like? How would they feel? Is there music we cannot hear? How would it sound? And ultimately, if we were able to enter such a magical place, how would we describe the experience to others? Did I mention I was a serious child?

Today we encourage all questions from our children. I have wondered what causes a shiver of disdain to creep up many spines when words such as "goddess" and "pagan" are mentioned? Our history is replete with stories of historical tyrants who instilled terror in the hearts of Jews, and who over the millennia have sought our destruction. Their stories we tell, we own, and we question, despite the horrific memories that the telling brings. What then was so dreadful about goddess-worshiping pagans that we still remain negatively conditioned, silent and inwardly recoiling from some unspoken memory? Why is this aspect of pre-patriarchal history still so deeply embedded in the Shadow?

In a startling book for its time, Merlin Stone wrote of the forgotten time in her book, *When God Was A Woman,* published in 1976. Revolutionary in its day, it was the forerunner of a body of work dealing with this theme. Was God once a woman? Is God now a man? No more and no less. I am always amused at the reaction of most Jews to this question. "Of course God is not male," they respond. "Well, in that case, how about changing the High Holy Day prayer next Rosh Hashanah and Yom Kippur from "our Father, our King" to "our Mother, our Queen?" Laughter always comes as a response.

The word "pagan" refers to someone connected to the land or the countryside. Describing someone as an *am ha-aretz* — a person of the Earth or land is a phrase that is now considered a put-down! Strange — or maybe not — for a people who were pastoral for so much of our early history. I understand that this form of "insult" came as we tried to distance ourselves from our unlettered past and elevated the importance of knowledge and literacy. Perhaps the time has come to rethink knowledge as only pertaining to academics. There is a wisdom that indigenous people have in their connection to the land that we have forgotten. Perhaps we need to remember there is much for us still to learn about our connections to Nature as part of the Oneness of creation.

Just as the forbidden fruit yields the sweetest juice, can we assume that forbidden questions will yield the most fascinating discoveries? Being Jewish, I ask questions. Being Jewish, I also answer with questions: How can we find out?

Our Father's House: The Coming Of The Patriarchy

As mentioned earlier, according to Eisler and other scholars, around seven thousand years ago, the archeological finds indicate that the harmony of the utopian setting of creative, egalitarian communities was disrupted. The question is why, how and by whom?

Perhaps marauding tribes from the northern reaches of Asia swept southwards in continuous waves. Their lives made difficult by climatic extremes, they continuously roamed the northern plains in search of pasturage for their herds. A warrior sky god was their deity. We can picture these ferocious warriors, mounted on horseback and feel the terror they would have instilled in those who possibly had never seen a rider mounted on a horse before. Were rider and animal thought to be one creature?

In their search for new pastures, they conquered the peaceful communities in their path. Considering those they overcame as inferior peoples of the land, they wanted to impose their culture on those they subjugated. Symbolically speaking, the imposition of their God would dethrone the Goddess and ultimately would lead to Her disappearance.

Removed in time and space from these events, contemporary women wonder why their foremothers ever gave up a culture in which they simultaneously celebrated their personal rights and their religious rites. Women probably held on as best they could, then were overpowered and forced into subjugation against their will. The Sacred Feminine went underground. She became concealed. The work of Gimbutas, Eisler and other scholars gives contemporary women a glimpse of a possible past of which we may be totally unaware. We begin to understand that patriarchy may not have been the only way human beings have ever interacted with one another; neither is it one that we have to continue. Once we can imagine a different and egalitarian society, we can create it. These scholars give us the invaluable gifts of possibility, potential, and promise.

Schlain suggests it was an "inside job" — that the advent of literacy hastened the demise of the Goddess. Reading and writing favored the development of the left-brain and its rational, logical reasoning over a meditative, artistic interpretation of reality, valuing the left-brain approach to life and a patriarchal paradigm. He suggests that the shift in consciousness came from within the human species rather than from an external enemy and that the development of literacy forced the Goddess to disappear from awareness.

History is always reported by the victors. We strain now to hear the silenced whispers of the voices of our foremothers recounting the tales of their lives in the peaceful agrarian settlements before the arrival of those pre-historic invading marauders. Our constriction of prehistoric time probably belies how long the process took. The changeover from pre-patriarchy to patriarchal times most likely took hundreds of years. From the evidence found, archeologists believe that these continuous waves of intruders from the north drastically altered the way of life in the southern arena of Asia Minor. Eisler reminds that we should not assume that the pre-patriarchal period was matriarchal — there are other forms of non-hierarchical community. She postulates a partnership model.

From this change-over period onwards, archeologists find

remnants of walled villages, often built on higher ground for protection and surveillance, fortified against enemies, with weaponry, slavery, and different types of burials for men of elevated rank, as compared to most men and all women. It would thus seem that a different and hierarchically classed society replaced a more egalitarian lifestyle, leaving precious little about the earlier way of life.

We turn to the study of mythology for keys to our prehistoric past. Earliest stories feature the Great Goddess. Where Divinity was worshipped as female, women, as her representatives, were held in high esteem. As the marauding tribesmen from the north subjugated the partnership-based villages in Southern Europe and Asia Minor, their warrior sky god dethroned The Great Goddess in her many forms, known to the people who worshipped Her as a creative and nurturing Divinity. Symbolically decapitated and diminished, Her worship was forbidden, although some may have continued worshipping Her in secret.

From the mythology of civilizations like the Ancient Greek and Roman, we see The Great Goddess deposed to the rank of consort to the male God. She wielded less power and importance, secondary now to her male counterpart. The earliest myths about the Great Mother and her son were replaced by tales of a younger God who took precedence over his aging mother. In Sumerian mythology, we read the story of the death of the Goddess Tiamat, the great Sky Serpent at the hands of her son. By slicing her in half to make the heaven and the earth he became the king of all the gods. The tale of her death may symbolically explain the triumph of the patriarchy over the ancient Goddess in much the same way as later Greek mythology elevated the status of the male gods on Olympus.

It is interesting how this mirrors Shlain's thinking. We can see the changing of the gods within, as the newer functions of the left-brain and its language centers overpower the importance of images and the right brain. Logic, sequential thinking, and analysis, began to dominate our perception and became the only valued way of perceiving our environment and evaluating our experiences.

The older emotional, intuitive perception of the right-brain with its focus on imaging, synthesis, and a cyclical under-standing of our world was overpowered and, like the Great Goddess, was deposed. The Sacred Feminine, like "Sleeping Beauty," fell asleep for thousands of years. Can we expect a "happily ever after" for humanity as She awakens, as foretold in the fairy tale? Did She remain with us, hidden within our fairy tales as the Fairy Godmother who magically assists us in times of need?

Long after the disappearance of the Goddess and the devel-opment of the image of Divinity as male, ancient oral tales remembered the primordial Goddess. These oral legends formed the essence of what was to become the mythic biblical tales in Genesis and Exodus, written and edited thousands of years later without direct and sanctified reference to Her. Qualities both masculine and feminine were combined within a single God.

Whatever remained of Goddess worship was denigrated as the cultic and forbidden practices of neighboring clans. As Her memory faded from consciousness, people in western culture were conditioned to react negatively both to the concept of "goddess" and to the "pagans" who still kept her memory alive. Women too were demonized, for example, in the stereotype of the witch, as men forgot the Goddess, so devaluing their own intrinsic feminine aspects. As we call back Her image from our individual Shadow worlds, we begin to recognize the Sacred Feminine for what She was, is and shall be, an integral image of Divinity for the whole human family, women in particular. Once the image of the Sacred Feminine reawakens we can help to restore Her dignity and that of women in society, restoring empowerment and hope for all in an inclusive society.

In the Ancient Near East, for thousands of years, She was worshipped in her different aspects as multiple goddesses, facets of the Great One, before the patriarchal influences turned that paradigm on its head. Then Divinity became worshipped as a single male God. Raphael Patai, in *The Hebrew Goddess* suggests that for many centuries after Sinai, goddess worship among Jews was part of religious life and powerfully attractive to both the leaders and the people. He reminds us that the goddesses *Asherah*, *Astarte*, and *Anath* were worshipped before and during the biblical period.

The Sacred Feminine may have been suppressed but lingers still within the pages of the Bible, the *Talmud*, and kabbalah. Gods are rarely "discovered" according to Patai; they are adopted by those who conquer, as we witnessed in the case of our ancestors in Canaan where *Asherah* was worshipped as Goddess. Her image was crafted as both tiny statuettes that could be held in the palm of the hand as well as larger wooden stakes that represented Her, a Nature Divinity, associated with growing trees. Her worship was a central feature of religious life in the times of the pre-monarchy, and King Solomon introduced Her worship into the Temple in Jerusalem.

Patai informs us that it is only post-exilic historians who look back and condemn the worship of *Asherah* as sinful. After the destruction of the first Temple, the exile to Babylonia was as shocking to the ancient psyche as the Holocaust was to us. At the time, the people must have asked themselves why, if they believed in the "One True God," He could have allowed his Temple to be destroyed? Some believed it happened because the people did not believe in Him enough and allowed goddesses into their places of worship. Conversely, others felt that worship of the Goddess was being neglected, as the male God became the primary form and face of Divinity. I speculate that this division occurred predominantly within the male and female halves of the community.

Contemporary Jews who believe that Judaism's gift to the world has always been the belief in one God are conflicted when learning that in the three hundred and seventy years of the Solomonic Temple, for two-thirds of its history, *Asherah* was worshipped as a legitimate part of worship. Over that three hundred year period, Her statue was brought in, removed for a time and returned continuously, remaining in place for one hundred years at one time. Patai informs us that written information about the worship of *Asherah* by biblical Hebrews recently came to light on two storage jars inscribed with the words, "May you be blessed by *Yahwe* and his *Asherah*." They were probably regarded as a Divine couple. *Asherah* is mentioned forty times in the Bible. After the destruction of the first Temple in the fifth century BCE, in the Egyptian colony, Patai reported, the Hebrews made donations to their gods: seventy to male gods, one hundred and twenty to female gods, and one hundred and twenty three to *Yahwe*.

All references in the text to tearing down the *asheras* and cutting down the trees — the natural settings of worship of the Goddess who was intimately connected with Nature — leaves no doubt about the agenda of the priests in that time-space continuum.

It is interesting too that in spite of the second commandment prohibiting graven images, in the first Temple, according to Patai, the Ark was guarded by cherubim. "Cherub" comes from the Hebrew word *K'rubh* which cannot be translated; the closest association is to the Akkadian *karibu* meaning an intermediary between humans and God.

Cherubs were the predominant religious leitmotifs in both the Tabernacle and the Solomonic Temple, which continued until its destruction in 70CE. According to Hellenistic Jewish authors, the ex-priest Josephus Flavius and the philosopher Philo, the *cherubim* may have caused some embarrassment. The priests would not want any association between these beings and the statues of gods and goddesses of local peoples. They did not want the presence of two *cherubim* to be interpreted as proof that the Jews did not worship a single and invisible God. To complicate the matter even further, a cherub representing the female principle could make mockery of the priests' condemnation of the Canaanite goddesses.

It has been further postulated that the two sacred stones in the Ark originally represented the male and female principles symbolized by *Yahwe* and his *Asherah*. With the development of the patriarchal image of One God, the female aspect was reduced to guardian of the Ark, as one of two cherubim. This is reminiscent of the demotion of the Great Goddess in Sumerian and Greek mythology. In Talmudic times, the male cherub became the symbol of God, the female cherub demoted to symbolize the people of Israel rather than the Sacred Feminine Herself. We see this relationship played upon in the Song of Songs, a celebration of a sensual relationship, a love story between God and His people. The Sacred Feminine goes into hiding within Judaism, dethroned, demoted and concealed, as in the other cultural heritages of ancient times.

For Jews then, the Sacred Feminine has always been within our teachings, concealed and waiting to be revealed as we mature beyond our spiritual adolescence. In coalescing the concept of multiple gods into the worship of a single God, She remains present within the unity of Divinity, waiting for us to see through the mystery.

Part Two: Thought

The Sacred Feminine Concealed

Who is wise? The one who learns from everyone.
From Pirke Avot, The Sayings of The Fathers

Left Brained Leanings

I am grateful for my religious upbringing for many reasons. Judaism teaches the importance of family, the significance of compassion, the beauty of prayer, the comfort of community, and the centrality of study. With The Student as a principal player on the stage of my inner life, I really love to learn. The Student confers with the Mystic in the struggles to understand.

My husband keeps reminding me, broad smile on that face I love, that I should be able to read without a pencil in my hand. My best-loved books are the ones on which my handwritten notes surround the text, resembling a page of Talmud — a passage of text in the middle of the page surrounded by comments and interpretations. When friends want to borrow any of my books, I have to warn them about my penchant for commenting on the text.

The love of learning is in the DNA of the Jew. Over the millennia, as we were forced to flee time and again, our ongoing study of our sacred texts became our homeland, portable and transferable from place to place as the need dictated. This most likely has kept the Jewish people viable in the face of tremendous odds. The focus of our study has always been our sacred texts.

Jews stand in awe before the Torah and its mysterious presence in our lives. We are filled with great emotion when we think of the extremes to which heroic individuals have gone in order to save the actual scrolls from damage or destruction and so preserve the ancient wisdom for future generations. As a woman, I have learned that I approach the teaching contained within the scrolls with a questioning attitude. What is the Torah, the *Tanach*, and the Talmud — our sacred literature, and what does it mean?

Central to Jewish life are collections of scrolls we refer to as *Tanach* — our Bible consisting of Torah — the Old Testament to those who are not Jewish — *Nevi'im* or Prophets and *Ketuvim* the name we give to a section of biblical tales referred to as The

Writings. From an ongoing study of these texts Jews draw values, morals and ethics, goals and aspirations. It is from an understanding of these texts that we believe the purpose of our lives is *tikkun olam* — the imperative to heal the brokenness of the world. From the texts is learned the importance of compassion as the guiding principle of our interactions with one another, the guidance to do no harm. From The Student and Mystic within, come the ideas and images that shape our understanding of Divinity, and the mutual sacred covenant into which we enter.

More specifically, Torah consists of the Five Books of Moses – Genesis, Exodus, Leviticus, Numbers, and Deuteronomy — the major focus of Jewish sacred literature. In addition to Torah, The Prophets or *Nevi'im*, from Joshua to Malachi, and the Writings, *Ketuvim* — the books of Psalms, Proverbs, Job, Song of Songs, Ruth, Lamentations, Ecclesiastes, Esther, Daniel, Ezra, Nehemiah, and Chronicles are studied. The Apocrypha is considered an addendum.

Above all, the Torah is mysterious — in its authorship, its grammar and structure, its imagery and stories, multi-layered with many possible interpretations. An effort to understand its mysteries increases the size of Judaism's library with the recorded discussions of the rabbis who debated the meaning of the texts long after the destruction of the Temple in 70 CE. These discussions were compiled in the form of the *Talmud* — interpretations of the Torah texts. Talmud, legalistic in nature, is referred to as *Halachic* literature. The more narrative interpretative material, the *Aggadic* texts are referred to as *Midrashic*. The former can be seen to reflect the literal left-brained approach to the texts while the latter is more metaphoric and symbolic — created in a storytelling format. As contemporary issues challenge the formulation of ethical responses, ongoing commentaries are offered as *Responsa* literature constantly written and updated, right up to the present moment. Just as the yearbook of any encyclopedia updates its information, *Responsa* material keeps updating views and values in the light of contemporary issues meeting ancient wisdom — all based on Torah and Talmud.

The Curiosity of Eve

The biblical Eve, as described in my *midrash* in the appendix, represents the curiosity with which all human beings are blessed. Understanding Eve as a creative energy rather than a physical woman, we realize that we can bless her (our nascent curiosity) for without her initiative, the human journey would not have begun. By dancing in Eve's footsteps, I honor my own curiosity that motivates me to follow the call of the mysterious.

There are many scholarly books by rabbis and academics explaining and interpreting our texts. My imagination is energized by a fascination with those elements that leave us perplexed — possible interpretations of the material that are edgy and challenging to interpret as we are so far removed from the telling of the original tales. Such texts and their possible interpretations often tend to be glossed over, giving more time to pursue the more obvious threads that lead to the historical growth and development of the Jewish people in covenant with Divinity. I acknowledge with gratitude the profound contribution being made by contemporary women, particularly those whose passion is mythic and mystical. Now included at the study table, women's voices are adding to the ongoing conversation with the ancient texts and its current interpretation.

Women's curiosity, participation and perspective bring new insights for consideration. Are we the Eves of modernity? Do we now question the patriarchal nature of the texts exactly as intended, just as Eve took the fruit from the Tree as she was meant to do in order to move humanity's story forward? Is the reluctance of some to reinterpret the texts (and the patriarchal structure that flows from its literal reading) the same "no-no" implicit in the instruction not to eat the fruit of the Tree of

Knowledge — the precise impetus to ensure we will do so? Throwing caution to the wind, listen for the drumbeat, join the dance and see where such questions can lead.

The magnificent poetry in the book of Genesis tells a story of order from chaos. Within the text, we follow the evolution of a people in covenant with Divinity, the implied goal of the experiential journey. Judaism believes that the world is incomplete and we are here to help complete it; just as we need Divinity, Divinity needs us as the agents of completion through whom God experiences the material world. I marvel at the humanness of the biblical characters who, like us, are all flawed persons — no perfected beings in this earthly tale! Rather we read the stories of the lives of dysfunctional families, characters with motives and agendas that they devise and carry out — as we do. From this amalgam we try to create an evolving ethic and morality about living with, and caring for other human beings and the Earth. We devise codes of behavior that encourage us to live up to our highest potential.

The Ancient Near East was the nursery in which the seeds of these biblical tales took root. The writing came centuries after the telling. It is believed that these oral stories were first part of several different traditions. It is likely that our contemporary interpretations of these ancient stories may fall far short of what was originally intended and easily understood at that time. However, the texts do still talk to us, even if in "accents" difficult for us to comprehend because of the time span between their original telling and the present. Do we credit the texts themselves or the genius of contemporary thinkers for the ability to continuously converse with these ancient words in an ongoing conversation, crossing barriers that distance both in time and space may suggest? In paradoxical fashion, the answer is yes to both alternatives.

This compendium of knowledge, our portable homeland has helped us survive our history of continuous settlement and expulsion. In his lyrical work, *The Spell of the Sensuous,* David Abram poetically describes the texts and the relationship of the community to the written word. The ancient Hebrews, he shares, were among the first communities to use a phonetic language to record more than just economically important record-keeping — a practice in many other parts of the world. They used the written language for passing on their mythology, stories, rituals, traditions, and laws, and in so doing, the written letters, rather than the land, carried the wisdom of the ancestors. A move from a spatial to a temporal focus expanded our understanding of history in terms of separation and movement.

This ability to move from the ancestral land with a portable wisdom enabled traditions to remain intact — vital, considering the experience of continual expulsion and exodus. Will the same serve the plight of Tibetan Buddhists who were forced from their homeland within our lifetimes? Will their texts help them survive in new and strange places? Do their texts hold the same place of importance in their religious and spiritual lives? Will the truths of their faith allow them to live meaningful lives and at the same time bring this wisdom to others who may otherwise not be exposed to the tenets of Tibetan Buddhism? The present Dalai Lama has posed this question to contemporary rabbis.

Mystery Abounds

The Mystic within me delights in the fact that the Torah scrolls are full of mystery. They are treated with great reverence. Complex, subtle, layered and beguiling they continue to call to us to solve the unknowable ambiguities revealed and concealed within them. One of my favorite books on the subject is Rabbi Lawrence Kushner's *River of Light.* This imaginative and mystical storyteller suggests that the Torah is but a fragment of the collective dream of the Jewish people. Just as dreams haunt us, the Torah tantalizes us. We can't explain it but we cannot stop trying. Just as with a dream, we honor its inscrutibility even if we do not immediately understand its symbolic wisdom. It is, he tells us, a multi-layered, idiosyncratic system of time and space.

> In both Bible and dream, nothing is accidental . . . the characters and even the very words and letters themselves are contorted, convoluted, condensed, inverted, rearranged, and often out of place. But we do not dismiss such a dream. Both Bible and dream are creations from the innermost depths of our collective and individual beings. Creations of our ancient memories of holy history that seem to hint at the ultimate nature of reality. *From River of Light.*

At the outset then, we know that as we approach Torah study we are about to dive into the depths of mystery of the sacred story-time realm of *Kairos.* The inner child loves a story; the adult within searches for meaning. Feminine nature responds to the intuitive, masculine temperament to the logical. As individuals, we are composites of the children we were and the adults we have become. Our temporal physical bodies house the immortal spiritual essence of who we are, as the masculine and feminine aspects of our beings interweave the fabric of our lives. The Torah beckons to us on all of these levels.

How do we attempt to intuit or understand the many layers and their hidden meanings? How do we grasp the wispy, ephemeral threads of fleeting images that form as we read the words. What beckons from beyond the borders of our conscious awareness?

On the most mundane level, the mystery of the texts begins with not knowing where chapters begin and end. The present chapter divisions were decided on years after the texts were written — in fact, in or around the thirteenth century B.C.E. Not only the chapters, but the endings of paragraphs are a matter of interpretation and differ in various versions of the texts, not reflected in the English translation.

As with the chapter endings, there are questions about where verses end because the scrolls contain neither punctuation marks nor vowels. Ambiguities exist with the words — starting with the first word of Torah — the Hebrew word *Bereishit*. Each translation is a portal to a different layer of meaning.

Another intriguing aspect of ancient Biblical Hebrew is the sense of time in the text with the use of what is called the *"vav reversive."* The Hebrew letter *vav* (V) normally understood to mean the word "and" is additionally used in biblical Hebrew as a device to change certain verb forms from present to past and past to present. This gives the text a timelessness in its very structure. For any contemporary traveler, the Gideon Bible is found in most hotel rooms. In its preface is the following statement: "Consecution of the tenses in Hebrew remains a puzzling factor in translation." The source for the Gideon Bible's statement is Rudolf Kittel's *Biblia Hebraica.*

We think of *Chronos* time as linear, moving inexorably from some distant point of our beginnings towards infinity. Earlier cultures, and possibly those that remain tied to the land today, understood time as circular rather than linear — as a continuous sweep of the repeating cycle that has neither beginning nor end. Focus on the annual cycle of seasons rather than the clock gives our lives a looseness that clock-watching does not permit. Problems often occur in contemporary life when Westerners attempt to make linear-timed appointments with tribal members whose ideas of time remain circular. I find it fascinating that the use of this "vav reversive" in the Torah allows for both linear time and cyclical time in its reading. Both the reading of history and the reading of myth within its texts is what biblical scholar Brevard Childs suggests:

Time stems ultimately from one primeval act of power before which there was no time and beyond which one cannot pass. This dividing line which separates the world of being from that of non-being marks off the beginning of time. There is no actual distinction in mythical time between the past, the present and the future. Although the origin of time is projected into the past, to the primeval act of becoming, this is only a form in which an essentially timeless reality is clothed. Time is always present and yet to come . . . . Mythical time is in no sense homogenous but, depending upon the quality of a particular time, is designated as holy or profane.

In opposition to modern historical thinking, which understands the future as growing out of the past but never repeating itself, the myth envisages the future as a return to the past. There is a complete disregard for chronological time since there is no true beginning or end. *From Myth and Reality in the Old Testament*

Child's comments about time in this ancient document becomes all the more intriguing in the light of quantum physics, which suggests that the physical world does not in fact operate in the way, for past centuries, we thought it did; time and space may not necessarily operate in the linear function our left-brain reasoning would have us believe. The Hebrew texts, written after the establishment of the patriarchy, could have discarded the concept of cyclical time in favor of the linear. The ability to read and write may have required a fixation on linear skills for human evolution; however, it does not negate that for thousands of years, time was understood as being cyclical and this may still have validity. Perhaps the paradox we need to understand is that we may chose to see time as both linear — leading from one event to another — and at the same time, cyclical or spiraling into space, hence the use of *Chronos* and *Kairos* is helpful.

Modern readers deal with a text that is puzzling, ambiguous, and ancient. As we can no longer access the culture and mindset in which these tales were told, we cannot possibly understand all the nuances. This makes its understanding complex. As we stand in awe of the miracle of the survival of the written word, we can wonder where we would be as a civilization if our sacred texts had never been written, but instead were told in the form of sacred stories to be memorized and handed down from generation to generation. This cultural practice saved the indigenous Moken people during the Tsunami of 2004. Members of an ancient fishing community in Thailand and Malaysia, they are well acquainted with the ocean and her many moods. Their legends and myths are continuously passed on as an oral tradition. On that fateful December day, when the ocean dramatically retreated further back than it had ever been known to do in contemporary times, Moken myths and legends warned the people of what was to come and as a group, they immediately came ashore and moved into the hills. Their folklore saved an entire community.

Writing freezes and preserves information, transforming flowing organic images into fixed concepts. Philosopher Marshall McLuhan, creator of the phrase the "medium is the message" reminded us that the form of communication we choose will affect the way the message is received. What happens then to the poetic ideas we try to share? Poetry, the language of the soul, is meant to be symbolic and metaphoric rather than literal. If we don't understand that the voice of the poet runs through some of the biblical text, particularly in the early books, it is no wonder we are plagued with misunderstandings and puzzled by seemingly illogical incidents as we try to translate the Bible as a literal reading. Stories are composed of three elements — the teller, the listener, and the story itself, most readily in sync when all three are in the same time-space continuum.

Here we are, thousands of years later, in societies and cultures drastically different from those of the ancient past. We have these mysterious scrolls from a time and place that is so foreign. As contemporary readers, how do we understand the words and the ideas they represent? For those who do not believe the Bible is the literal word of God, there is a need to consider first and foremost the authors of the text as we try to unravel some of its enigma. Who were they and what were their goals in writing? What skills had the earliest writers developed that brought this material to life in a way that had not been done before?

Much of the information contained within the ancient scrolls is timeless, inspirational and poetic. Not so with everything. Many ideas are historic and from my perspective, may have been timely in ages past but are no longer appropriate to an evolving human consciousness. The text has survived and the Mystic within stands in awe that this amazing document is still available for all to reverently approach, and enter into dialogue, with it. The many "gaps" in the stories encourage questions to which there are no definitive answers, but multiple possibilities and limitless interpretations.

For me, the most significant aspect of the entire text is neither the law, nor the history, mythology and poetry, but the images and concepts of Divinity that are contained within the tradition. In order to understand ourselves, we need to understand the God to whom we pray. We can look around our "global village" brought into our homes daily via the internet and television and see many different images of Divinity which exist today. These images provide an insight into the nature and values of the communities who ascribe to these diverse understandings. The contemporary fundamentalist view of a judgmental Father appeals to those whose values are very different from the ecologists who understand Divinity as a loving presence in Nature.

We are told that we were created in that Divine image. If so, what does that mean? Do we create Divinity in images that relate to who we are in space and time? Such images in no way change or affect the nature, reality, or attributes of The Creative Source of All Life, but rather tell us about who we are and to what we aspire.

There are many ways to read the text. Those who choose to

read the Bible literally face the great dilemma of the nature of Divinity portrayed as jealous, petulant, and a very human father figure. Perhaps we can accept this image more readily if we acknowledge that biblical stories were written for a community in transition — in their spiritual infancy, as the term "children of Israel" would literally suggest. In their initial stages of development and cohesion as a unified people, the authoritarian, human-like Father-figure God may have been fitting. Centuries later, moving from our spiritual childhood to adolescence and early adulthood, we need to ask if this image still works for us. Perhaps we need to find new images for the same Divine energy.

Writing the Bible

Twenty-first century American women come to the texts with several decades of feminism to bolster and support inquiry. Aware of the contemporary milieu, educated women come to the table with different beliefs and experiences. Some Jews believe that the Torah was written by Moses; many believe the texts were written between the twelfth and second century B.C.E. What do we know about the authors of the material?

The Documentary Hypothesis, formulated by Julius Willhausen at the end of the nineteenth century, suggests that through the repeated use of certain words and phrases, we can trace several different sources of biblical text. In his book *Who Wrote the Bible* Richard E. Friedman helps us understand the differing J, E, P, D and R schools or biblical strands. Source J uses for Divinity, the term *YHVH* — the name for God that Jews do not know how to pronounce and non-Jews pronounce as Jehovah or Yahweh. This source is thought to be the oldest. Source E, relatively short, probably comes next chronologically. E uses the term *Elohim* for God's name. J and E sources represent the most ancient information — through them, we can discern the mythic and poetic voice of the text. Their ancient stories, particularly those from Genesis and Exodus, came from different time periods, possibly separated from each other by long spans of time. They are selected versions of oral traditions that may date back hundreds if not thousands of years prior to their being recorded in history. If one listens to the ancient whispers from the sacred texts, we sense tangible differences in the feel of these older tales, when compared to the authoritarian voice of the priests who were charged with building a sacred community at a much later time in history.

Source P is the voice of the Priests, using *Elohim* and other names, but never *YHVH*. Did they know to be true what Rabbi Mark Sameth suggests about this name discussed in the section entitled "The Who-ness and What-ness of God?" Within the parameters of their political and priestly agendas, they tried to impose control on the hearts and minds of the people they were attempting to unify. At the same time, their wish was to separate these people from what they considered the surrounding and corrupting influences of other cultures. Most important, from their perspective, were the issues pertaining to God's presence in the community and, as a prerequisite, the need for order and purity. It is thought that the P source was active both before and after the Babylonian exile of 586 BCE.

There are two more sources described by Friedman — the Deuteronomic source known as D, responsible for most of the Book of Deuteronomy, similar to the P source, but written in varying literary styles. Finally Source R is the Redactor – the person or persons whose task it was to weave these stories together in a tapestry that would become one, and represent the whole.

To complicate the matter, not only are there different sources but we can trace the work of several sources within single stories. In the past we believed that repeating themes in a single story were a form of emphasis, just as the command "bold" is on the computer. Alternately, these repetitions may result from the blending of variations on a single theme, consciously woven together — perhaps to satisfy different groups who were being forged into a single people, the presumed goal of the R source. Their oral histories had favored different versions of mythic or archetypal stories. To be inclusive, the editors of the texts may have included and interwoven these differences into the final version of the Bible.

By referring to Friedman's book, it is easy for any contemporary reader to learn the source of any lines in the text. With this perspective, biblical reading takes on a new dynamic.

The Torah, as a story of our history, reads as a God-centered tale rather than an historical account. There are no historical records that would corroborate the actual existence of Abraham and Sarah, Rebecca and Isaac, Jacob, Leah, Rachel or Joseph. Neither have we any historically verifying account of a Moses. In fact, in the extensive literary history of the Egyptians, there is no proven evidence of an extended sojourn of the ancient Israelites in Egypt, suggesting that this story may have more of a mythic base than an historic one. Some scholars suggest that the *Hyksos*, who according to Egyptian sources were expelled from Egypt, may have been the ancient Hebrews.

It is believed by many today that the story of the Exodus, of such primary importance to the Jewish people, may have been adopted from a mythic motif of the experience of a small group, possibly the *Hyksos*, who became part of the newly forming Israelite tribes in the area that is today Israel. The power of the story from slavery to freedom was strong enough then, as it is today, to be considered of seminal importance. It is the symbolic story of humankind.

Although archeology has confirmed some of the text, towards the end of the twentieth century archeologists began discovering evidence that contradicted Biblical information previously thought of as historical. If we remember that this text is supposed to be a story about our developing relationship with God, it is not that important for archeology to support it.

The Bible then is our history, our mythology, and our inspired poetry, written by different people at different times with different goals. Most problematic and challenging for me, the Bible is our left-brain connection to Divinity. Does its naming and description of Divinity fit our personal understanding of the God to whom we pray in the sanctuaries of our own souls? How do we image the Source of All Life that we address in our prayers? Does the image remain constant when our prayers are pleas from our troubled hearts in times of challenge compared to the times when they are recitations of gratitude and appreciation?

Reading the Bible

As we have seen, the ability to read and write is a relatively recent achievement of the human family. Only ten thousand years ago, we began to use the written mark as more than an iconic or artistic symbol. New neurological patterning that would allow these abilities to function had to evolve. Words are the tools we use to describe our experience; as symbols of the reality they represent, they express ideas, thoughts, feelings, beauty and love, allowing us to share the wonders of our lives. At the same time, the ability to use hate words that tear down, destroy, and hurt can ultimately lead to genocide. Explosive power is contained in these sounds or letters strung together as symbols for reality.

As symbols, they should never be taken as more than that and should never entice us into the worship of the word, written or spoken. Worship of any "part" for the whole is idolatry. For example, the worship of any symbol of Divinity, instead of Divinity itself, is idolatrous. This can apply to the words we use as well. We need to remember that no symbol is ever the reality for which it stands. We are reminded of that beautiful Buddhist saying about a finger pointing at the moon. If we concentrate on the finger we miss the marvel of the moon itself, and miss the fact that the purpose of the extended finger was to direct our attention elsewhere.

In biblical study, as we seek the Truth with a capital T, we want to refrain from the idolatry of worshipping the literal, concrete word for the flowing reality it represents. Accepting only a literal reading of the text can be seen as idolatrous reading. It will deny the reader the opportunity to remain open to all possibilities and potentials that may be layered within the text.

Enslavement to the literal reading of the Bible has brought misunderstanding and untold hardship to millions around the world. I think of the Dutch Reform Church of South Africa and its endorsement of *apartheid* based on their interpretation of the Bible; it was the basis of their pronouncements of who should be servant to whom. I wonder what the original storytellers would feel — seeing the turns and twists their thoughts and words have taken since being written.

As we open to the possibilities of diverse cultures and civilizations that operated differently from ours, we begin to acknowledge a fuller and more complete picture of the past and of ourselves, and therefore our future potential. The existence of the texts, as eternally mysterious and incomplete as they are, with all the problems that they bring, have certainly given and continue to give scholars wonderful material to work with, to debate, to challenge, to inspire, and to reinterpret over the millennia.

Questioning The Bible

I bring a questioning attitude to the texts. As symbols, words are channels to our relationship with religion, spirituality and ultimately with Divinity. I cannot help but relate to them according to their "feel." For some, the main interest in the sacred literature is the study of Jewish history and the legal system that evolved for building a holy community. I am most profoundly conscious of the hand of humanity in this aspect of the texts.

Elements such as these do not resonate with me as a connection to Divinity. While it is interesting to read from an historic perspective, these words do not inspire me. Laws are constructed to create community. Devising laws in the name of God enhances the power of the priests and at the same time, diminishes the transcendent image of Divinity. The resulting discrimination and separation within the community itself as well as the judgmental and chauvinistic attitude towards others does not feel like Divinity for me. If we honor our feelings and intuitions in the same way as we do our thoughts, surely these senses are vitally important avenues for our understanding of God.

In contemporary times, we witness and are appropriately skeptical of the many self-appointed prophets who claim to know what God wants for us. Some end as did Jim Jones, founder of the People's Temple. Evangelical ministers vociferously inform us that they know what God wants for the world; however, their messages are invariably exclusivist and judgmental, removed from the grand Divine design that surely teaches the centrality of unity in diversity. Irrespective of how loudly these self-appointed agents of Divinity shout, and despite however many naïve or misguided individuals they may attract, their beliefs remain exclusivist, and from my perspective, are doomed to fade into the approaching sunset of the old order. As I write this book, we are starting to see how the issue of ecology and our role in global warming is beginning to strain the unity of the evangelical Christian community as Mother Nature begins to stir in our midst. Bill Moyers' program "Is God Green?" showed some the division between the liberal and fundamentalist strains in the Christian community in this regard. I personally look at the injunctions of the ancient priests in the same vein as I try to sort, by feel, the purpose of their words. I celebrate my intuitive sense as a valued friend at the study table.

Breath and The Bible

I know that I am not alone in sensing connections to Divinity in some biblical texts and not in others. David Abram, in his book, *The Spell of the Sensuous*, poetically suggests there are passages in the text in which the "breath of the Divine" feels absent. He uses the term Divine "breath" as the force that brings the ancient words to life. He reminds us that the text was transcribed with consonants only. There were no letters for the vowels. The function of a consonant is to stop or modulate the flow of air or breath, in Hebrew, *ruach*, while vowels are used to add voicing to the unimpeded breath-stream; together the consonants and the vowels create the divine dance of stop and start that makes human speech the miracle it is.

In this fashion, Abram suggests that the breath of the reader brings the written consonants to life, just as the archetypal "earthlings" Eve and Adam, were animated by Divine *ruach* or breath as described in the Book of Genesis, translated in the Hertz Pentateuch:

Then the Lord God formed man of the dust of the ground, and breathed into his nostrils the breath of life; and man became a living soul. Gen 2:7

We can translate this same sentence in this fashion:

Then The Wholly One formed humanity of the dust of the earth, and breathed into their nostrils the breath of life, and the human being became a living soul. Gen 2:7

Abram suggests the permanent, written inclusion of the vowels may have been seen as creating a "visible likeness of the divine," which the ancient Hebrews would not do, forbidden as they were to create any likeness of the Divine in visual form. There needed to be an interaction between the reader and the text in order to bring the letters to life. Just as the earthling was awaken to life by the divine breath, inanimate letters similarly need the breath to become animate. This would ensure the conscious awareness and presence of the reader at all times in conversation with the text itself.

Without a record of which vowel would be appropriate in each word, the reader selects from a series of possibilities. In English we know that differences in meaning change the possibilities that exist between any two consonants — for example, between "b" and "n" we find the words ban, Ben, bin, bun, bane, been, bean, bone, and boon. Each of these versions of the b-n possibilities will lead to very different conclusions in a sentence.

The relationship of vowels, the breath and the connection to Divinity is the fascinating subject of many authors, particularly those interested in meditation and the breath of life. Rabbi Alan Lew in his book, *Be Still and Get Going*, states that while the rest of creation came into being by the word of God, humanity receives the breath of Divinity. No wonder we are entreated to honor our ability to breathe, an involuntary process that we take for granted. The breath that calms us is a powerful aid to meditation. Abram states that the "most sacred of God's names would thus seem to be the most breath-like of utterance — a name spoken as it were, by the wind." The name he refers to is the Tetragrammaton, the YHVH. He reminds us that some kabbalists propose that the YH can be likened to a whispered drawing into the body of the breath of life, and the VH the unvocalized flow of the breath as it leaves the body.

Alice O. Howell, quotes Jungian analyst and author Edward C. Edinger in her book, *The Heavens Declare*:

"the consonants of the Hebrew alphabet were derived from looking at the pattern of the stars, and.. the planets are the vowels moving in and out of the consonants, thereby writing the endless story of life."

The poetic beauty of these ideas moves me deeply. They confirm a fascination with the magic of the letters that we use to manipulate and understand our environment, giving us some feeling of power over the ever-unfolding world of experience. In this way, words are indeed magical and may be confusing.

As in other languages, many words in Hebrew have different meanings. *Ruach* means Spirit and also wind — the connection to the breath is easy to see. *Avodah* means work or worship. We can view the relationship between the two meanings. Work can become an act of worship when we approach our labor with an awakened consciousness, bringing the best that is within us to each circumstance and situation. *Avodah* can also imply that it takes concentration and focus to worship effectively. Unless we bring our full attention to the words we use in prayer, they are nothing but words. With our energy engaged, the words can lift us to a different dimension and by working in this way, our prayer or worship becomes an organic link with Divinity.

Mysticism and The Bible

Every religious tradition has an outer, rather rigid façade that is easily recognized by practitioners of the faith. Like a mask from ancient Greek theatre, sometimes it is the mask of tragedy, at other times, the mask of comedy; all religions mask in some way the inner, organic impulse, the esoteric teaching that animates the outer shell.

The exoteric façade can be likened to an ornate metal lantern. The rituals and dogmas that differentiate religions from one another can be compared to the glass inserts that adorn the lantern frame, each different in color and design. The inner flame of Divinity burns brightly in the center of the lamp. It may not be as easily recognized by all, but glows from a universal fire of spiritual truth.

Every religious tradition attempts to answer the age-old questions: who am I, why am I here, and where am I going? Islam has sufism, Christianity, mysticism, and Judaism has kabbalah. Traditionally, to study kabbalah, a Jew had to be forty years old, male and well-versed in Torah. Now the public suddenly seems to be aware of, and more curious about this ancient body of knowledge. It took a Shirley Maclaine to make reincarnation dinner-table conversation. Madonna's interest in Jewish mysticism has made people who may otherwise never have been interested, suddenly wanting to know more about kabbalah. We can't help but smile when we realize it is two women who have sparked the debate; and the name of the latter heightens the amusement.

The Bible may contain allegories and stories that are historical in nature; the kabbalah uses images and allegories that are timeless. The inner mystical aspect of Judaism is used to reinterpret the biblical themes from a more universal perspective because it feeds from the ancient and timeless source of *Kairos*, the repository of spiritual and universal laws and lore. How do mystics then read and interpret the text in ways that may seem magical, metaphoric, mythic, and mysterious to our left-brained logical selves?

Mystics have suggested a number of ways in which the text is a holy Mystery. It has even been suggested that all the letters of the Torah when joined together are one continuous name of God. Certainly from the human perspective, for anyone who first realizes that marks on a page carry meaning and symbol, magic abounds. Much has been made in Jewish mysticism of the power and magic of each individual letter and the meanings that can be read not only into the words they spell, but the numerical value of each word. In Hebrew, the study of *Gematriah* teaches that every letter, representing not only a sound or a segment of an alphabet, is also a numeral as well. This allows us to read biblical Hebrew in another way entirely.

Aleph is "a" and 1, *bet* is "b" and 2 and so on. Combinations of letters can be read as words or as numerical symbols, and can be linked to other words of similar numeric value. *Ha Teva* (Nature) and *Elohim* (a name for Divinity) have the same numerical value. The numeric connections that dwell below the surface and hidden within the text, acknowledge of the sanctity of Nature.

There is an ancient mystical belief that by combining and recombining different permutations of the Hebrew letters, we can change our awareness. Author Myla Goldberg, based her book *Bee Season* on this idea. Anyone inexperienced and innocent (as symbolized by a naïve, young girl in this story) who tries to force a shift in conscious awareness can become un-grounded, pushed over the edge of reality and into mental instability.

Similar notions of the innate power of the Hebrew letters and their mystical combinations is a sub-theme of the futuristic novel *He, She and It* by Marge Piercy. Weaving ancient legends into a society in which artificial intelligence plays an important role, she recounts the familiar Jewish legend of the *golem*. The traditional figure of clay is brought to life by the incantations of knowledgeable rabbis, who reverently knew how to combine the powerful Hebrew letters to animate the inanimate. Piercy is able to blur the lines between where our humanity ends and artificial intelligence begins. We query the possibility of artificially created emotions and spirituality, and the ancient legend is read with new eyes.

Transition from one state to another is the province of a different field of metaphoric study, namely the magical realm of alchemy. Fred Allen Wolf, in his book, *Mind into Matter: a new alchemy of science and spirit*, writes that the ancient alchemists took their impetus from kabbalistic teaching. He suggests that within the sacred texts of Judaism was a hidden doctrine that actually explained the texts. The mysteries of kabbalah and alchemy have a common goal — the transformation to purity from the common or base. Much of the alchemist's belief was hidden in metallurgic concepts of making gold from base metals. Spiritually, they were, like the kabbalists, interested in transforming normal perception to the highest "golden" level.

Alchemy then was both a material and a spiritual process of transformation. Wolf states that the Hebrew letters themselves are powerful portals to the inner world beyond the borders of the religion itself. Kabbalists believed that through these symbolic doorways they could plunge into the universal code hidden beneath the surface of the text. In doing so they believed that as the letters became animate within them, they would open to new insights regarding spiritual and material existence.

So we find a fascination with the Hebrew letters themselves as well as their ordering in the text. Mystery revolving around the letters and the precise order in which they appear in the text, leads to interesting speculation. Michael Drosnin's book *The Bible Code* intimated that, in the light of holographic thinking and the teachings of quantum physics, hidden within the text was a code that could foretell a number of possible futures of the world. The method that was used was mathematical and the tool employed, the computer. The concept of many possible outcomes is basic to the field of quantum physics. The accuracy of this claim regarding the prognostication in biblical text is for readers of *The Bible Code* to consider. It is one view of many that the biblical texts are more than they first appear to be.

That there may be many ways of reading any line of text is basic to the kabbalistic approach. Like the ever-unfolding lotus, the more deeply we delve into the texts, the more nuances and shades of understanding bloom before our eyes. Mystics teach that the text can be read on four levels, *P'shat*, the literal, *Remez*, a hint at the metaphoric level, *Drash*, the broader reading of the allegorical, and *Sod*, the mystical, inner meaning. How does this operate?

We can look at the creation of humanity in the following four ways as we read deeper into the text of the story of Eve and Adam:

P'shat

On a literal level, God created Adam and Eve, one woman and one man, in a physical garden. The Hertz *Chumash* offers this translation:

> And God created man in His own image; male and female created He them. Gen 1:27

We can also translate the Hebrew as:

> And The Holy One created the earthlings in The Divine's own image; in the image of Divinity, The Holy One created them; male and female Divinity created them. Gen 1:27

From Genesis 2 we get another version of the creation of humanity, with Eve having been created from the rib of Adam. And in the opening chapters, inquiring minds come across one of the earliest problems with the text. Two versions – which one is true? Sumerian mythic scholar Zachariah Sitchin informs us that in the Sumerian myth that precedes our Bible, the word *"Ti"* meant both rib and life. Was this a pun by the early storytellers that we have now concretized as a literary fact? If we follow the second storyline as a literal reading of fact, with Eve being created from Adam's rib, we run into immediate problems. How can we understand this in light of what we know about human physiology? In the same literal vein, if Eve was the first mother and bore only sons, where did Cain's wife comes from? Literalist questions such as these back us into corners out of which there is seemingly no escape.

Biblical text goes on to describe Eve's "disobedience" as the cause for human hardship and suffering. We need to ask ourselves if the God we pray to requires obedience above all else? What does that say about the nature of Divinity? Why are we gifted with curiosity if we were not meant to use it to spur us on to take part in *tikkun olam* — to improve the broken-ness of the world?

Remez

A deeper reading of the text as symbolic will reveal a hint of something more than meets the eye. Perhaps we can say God created humanity as a duality — both male and female represented by the archetypal patterns — Eve, symbolic of Woman, in Hebrew, *isha* (*aleph-shin-hey*) and Adam, symbolic of Man, in Hebrew, *ish* (*aleph-yud-shin*). Common to both words are the letters *aleph* and *shin*, which forms the word *aish* — "fire." The Hebrew word for "man" adds the letter *yud* while the Hebrew word for "woman" adds the letter, *hey*. *Yud* and *hey* are the first two sounds of the Tetragrammaton, *yud-hey-vav-hey*, the unpronounceable name of Divinity, and source of the Christian use of the word Jehovah/ Yahweh.

There exists the potential for all human beings to experience both the masculinity of Adam (of the earth/earthling) and femininity of Eve (mother of all living things) as an animate spirituality in a material world symbolized as the Garden of Eden. The conscious experience of masculinity and femininity is blessed and sanctified when in balance as it draws *yud* and *hey* together in the "image" or symbol of Divinity that kabbalists describe as the unity of the Holy One and the *Shechinah*. Without the connection to *yud* and *hey*, their commonality is *aish* or fire that consumes the disconnected earthling Adam, *ha–adam* which could be translated as "of the Earth."

What do we understand by the terms masculinity and femininity? Masculinity is not 'power-over' through brute force; rather it is the use of physical strength with an appreciation of the way the elements in the material world operate for the sustenance of life.

Femininity could be considered as the spiritualizing or sanctifying of those actions, of layering symbolic meaning on to the daily tasks we perform. How do we define the terms masculinity and femininity today? Once defined, how do we form our goals and expectations of those characteristics in our lives for the benefit of the group? Connecting with Divinity may be the key.

Drash

At a deeper level yet, we can say that within our human bodies we carry male and female energies, the intellect and intuition, thought and feeling, doing and being — symbolizing the dualities or polarities of the material plane. Jung taught that the anima or female energy exists within all men, just as the animus, or male energy, is part of the patterning of every woman. At this level, Eve's decision to taste the fruit of the Tree of Knowledge is the intuitive aspect of ourselves that leads us forward to experience life. Tasting of the fruit of the Tree of Knowledge of Good and Evil, is a metaphoric expression for teaching us that as we live our lives, we constantly try to find a balance point between two polarities that exist in every aspect of our physical reality. Had she eaten of the Tree of Life instead of the Tree of Knowledge, physicality and duality would never have been tasted. At the very outset of our story, the possibility of choice existed. Two trees grew in the Garden.

Far from being disobedient, Eve's action in taking the fruit represents the intuitive self's understanding of exactly what was intended in the Divine Plan. My *midrash, Eve-olution: the birth of humankind* appears in the appendix at the back of the book. The story of the symbolic, forbidden Tree becomes a storyteller's device — hinting that the protagonists must take on the challenge of tasting the fruit to move the story forward. Thematically this device is used in many stories such as the fairy tale about the abusive nobleman BlueBeard and his curious wife or the Greek mythic character Pandora. BlueBeard's nameless wife is forbidden to enter one room in the chateau, which of course she enters only to find the bodies of Bluebeard's murdered wives.

Pandora's curiosity led her to open a container she was forbidden to open and so released all the world's troubles. We tell these tales to our children, where the characters are instructed not to do the very thing that needs to be done to make the story unfold. It is the impetus to travel the path that is offered if, and when, we are brave enough to take the challenge.

Sod

Is the secret revealed at this deepest of levels that Eve, Adam and the Garden of Eden never were — they always are. Eve, together with her partner Adam, spirituality and physicality, resides within each human being. Re-awakening and honoring the vital Eve energy within us, beckons us to cross the threshold of the surface time that is *Chronos* and enter the depths of *Kairos*.

At the mystical level, we answer the question whether we are human beings on a spiritual journey or spiritual beings on a human journey with a resounding "yes." We are both. We take on "garments of skin," the physical bodies we require to experience the material world, as we learn to balance the polarities that are part and parcel of physicality. Thinking back to the illustrations of my childhood Bible, I thought garments of skin were the pelts of slain animals!

On this journey of life and burgeoning consciousness, we have been given the gift of bringing spirituality into the material plane, as we transmute emotional experience back to our Source. We can choose to continue in the "either/or" paradigm of the past or find ways to view reality as a paradox and function within a "both/and" modality. We learn to unify rather than separate. Author and lecturer, Anne Wilson Shaeff's insight about paradigmatic change is most insightful. In her book *Women's Reality*, she is able to raise readers' consciousness and offers novel and creative alternatives and choices to be made in daily life. We have the option to see and recognize both the Divine commonality and human uniqueness that reside within each of us, and in that recognition, acknowledge and honor the same within The Other. Surely this is the challenge and goal of life as we learn to find the point of balance between unity and diversity and see them both as aspects of the Oneness of Divinity.

How long it takes each human being to awaken to this truth is a decision for each soul. We will all arrive at this awareness, but the length of the journey to recognition and remembrance is a soul choice.

Finally, as is done with a play on the magic of the letters and words in Hebrew, if we take the first letter of each of these words that subtitle the preceding sections — P'shat-Remez-Drash-Sod as P-R-D-S, we have the root of the Hebrew word *pardes* meaning orchard. Reminiscent of The Garden? Does this tell us, concealed within the meanings and nuances of metaphor and myth is the possibility that perhaps as we bring together all four levels of comprehension, we are ready to re-enter the Garden from whence we came and are finally able to bring godliness down to Earth? This a good example of the whole being far more than merely the sum of its parts.

Eve is. Adam is. The Garden of Eden is the present moment, the Garden to which we can return the instant we release the memory of the past and the anticipation of the future. If ready to cross that threshold, please join the dance.

Mythology and The Bible

The tales in the early stories of Genesis are told in the voice of the mythologist and have a very different feel to the voice of the priests in later sections. The word "myth" is understood in two different ways. In conversational speech, we refer to something untrue as myth. Here we turn to the more metaphoric understanding of myth that refers to a universal truth or wisdom — in the words of author Jean Houston, "something that never was and always is." We often find ourselves is situations that play out in mythic terms — a child forcibly taken from its mother can be seen as a replay of the Greek myth of Demeter and Persephone. Anyone who has lived through such a nightmare knows the organic truth of this mythic tale. Such real-life experiences allow us to marvel at the truth of mythic experiences as teachers, alerting us to closely attend to the power of mythic themes wherever they exist — in this case, to the mythic content of biblical stories.

The tale of the exodus from Egypt is a great example. Is the biblical account historical? A recent television documentary by director James Cameron, *The Exodus Decoded* suggests that the Egyptian plagues and the crossing of the Red Sea were linked to the volcanic explosion on the Greek island of Santorini three and a half thousand years ago. The idea is intriguing and similar to the work of Immanuel Velikovsky who wrote *Worlds in Collision* in 1965.

We describe the events of the exodus each year at Passover. The mythic base of the story is probably the real reason that the journey to freedom is as important and as powerful as it is — as timely as it is timeless, an event that "never was and always is."

A favorite mythic character in the Bible is Moses, with his alter-ego Aaron. The do-er in the physical world, he works together with his sister Miriam, the feminine intuitive sense. Are these characters three aspects of a single person? We have no historical proof there ever was a Moses but the journey of his life provides a profound teaching. Whether any of the events described ever actually happened is far less important than what we learn from the story.

From a mythic perspective, the life of Moses, as described in my *haggadah*, *Towards Freedom*, depicts the archetypal hero's journey. As a spiritual teaching, his odyssey holds one of the most important places in Jewish sacred texts specifically because of its archetypal relevance in the universal search for freedom. Once we dive beneath the surface of the literal meaning, we can reveal to conscious awareness the masked images and symbols of the story.

The archetypal Moses, estranged from his birth family, typical of the hero, finds himself in a foreign environment in which he comes of age. Forced from his everyday circumstances, he embarks on a journey — complete with mentors and threshold guardians — that takes him into the unknown; this odyssey presents him with enormous challenges, magical and miraculous. Ultimately, he returns from the abyss with a gift for humankind. In other faith traditions, could we read the life stories of Siddhartha Gautama—The Buddah, and Jesus of Nazareth in similar mythic vein? In Judaism, Moses, like all other biblical characters, is a flawed human being, rather than an *avatar* or *bodhisattva* — enlightened beings of Eastern traditions.

The story of the exodus from Egypt can be seen as a mystical map that can lead us out of the physical constriction of total reliance on the material world. When we step back from our everyday concerns we can try to find meaning in our lives. Then, like the ancient Israelites, we too wander through the unknown wilderness of inner worlds. Here, we can break our fixations with materialism and move towards the inner "promised land" — the place in which we obtain an insight about our true nature and our own relationship with Divinity.

Other mythic moments in the Torah are enlightening. Rabbi Michael Lerner taught that the events at Sinai where the Ten Commandments were received happen continuously as we center ourselves and still the noise of our busy lives to become present. Rabbi Lawrence Kushner teaches that the real miracle in the desert was not that Moses saw the burning bush remained unconsumed, but that he stood still long enough to notice.

Myth is metaphor and like all metaphors may be literally false on a superficial level, but as we delve below to a more substantive reality, they reveal themselves to be "profoundly true," says Professor Marc Brettler in his book *How to Read the Bible*. He goes on to state that if we wish to understand something of collective importance, it is through the interpretation of myth and metaphor that we approach the Truth. As we have become more left-brained and rational, we see the world as passive and impersonal. In earlier times, we understood our surroundings as active and alive, with powers that influence every area of life. Brevard Childs commented there was an openness and receptivity to these impinging forces made known to us in dreams and hallucinations that arose from the subconscious. Basic to the constructing of myth is the creative impulse of humanity as we attempt to order a multiplicity of impressions into a cohesive whole — from chaos, an order that we ascribe to the gods.

Living mythically requires us never to take for granted the apparent order in the world. Living symbolically is to be seen as part of the process of becoming. Myth is more than a story being told — it is a reality being lived. We understand its profundity when we feel it shift us from *Chronos* into *Kairos*. The mythic opening to the Torah indicates the shift. "In the beginning" can be understood as "once upon a time," which has the same unfolding quality of a story in progress.

Other mythic remnants in the biblical text continue to puzzle the rabbis. For example, like Jacob before him, Moses battled a stranger in the night. After the earlier incident Jacob is transformed, having confronted his demons and his name is changed to Israel, indicating he has wrestled with Divinity. In the Moses story, it is his wife, Zipporah who understands and immediately acts by circumcising her infant son and throwing the foreskin at Moses' feet, calling him a "bridegroom of blood." What can this mean?

Again, we have the image if not the voice of the Sacred Feminine intuitive sense at work. This is one of those stories that makes no sense to the modern reader. Whereas the original circumcision practice in other cultures was a puberty rite, here we see the infant being circumcised early to save the life of his father. Although there is no way of knowing for sure what the story means, it may be an example of ancient knowledge understood only by those who heard it at the time the tale was being told. It remains a mystery to us that beckons us to a deeper reading of the text.

Etymologists can show that some of the words used in the text were ancient even to the writers of the Torah. The scribes used explanations of what they meant by these words no longer used. An example is the word *nephilim* now understood to refer to giants.

We stand in wonder and awe of the ever-opening mystery of the texts from which springs the Jewish tradition. Its *Kairos* nature makes it timeless. That the texts remain open to continuous reinterpretation is perhaps one of the most enigmatic aspects of all. Layer after layer reveals intriguing inspiration, discussion, and insight on multiple levels. It speaks to us at whatever level we enter the dialogue. As a living document that the reader brings to life with its reading, like the Sacred Feminine, we sense its wonder and then mysteriously, acknowledge that a new insight is gleaned. Is it any wonder then that the very nature of Divinity Itself, revealed within these layers, expresses an ever-unfolding energy available to us at whatever level we approach, dependent on the stage of our own spiritual maturity? The voices of the mystics and mythologists in the discussion with these ancient scrolls will continue to elicit novel and meaningful insights that can enrich the lives of us all. With such an understanding of ancient wisdom, we know that it is possible for us to build a future of inclusivity that will replace the hierarchical societal structure of the past.

The Who-ness Or What-ness Of God

The Torah then is unfinished and like our universe, in process. Can we can say it is the first interactive text in human history? The words are left inanimate forever unless there is a reader. This is one text that is far from being a static document. Through its interactive design, it is organic. Each generation will bring new insights and questions to the text that keeps it, ourselves, and Divinity forever spiraling out into infinity. Jews believe the world, too, is incomplete and it is our task to repair the broken, to complete the unfinished that we have been given. This is the holy work of *tikkun olam*.

Just as there is an evolving text, with verbs that magically relate to time as both linear and cyclical in an evolving world, how perfect that we have been given an evolving name for Divinity too. Are not the three — the text, humanity, and Divinity — intimately related?

If we stop thinking of Divinity as a noun, that most fixed and boxed-in type of word, and start to think of God as a verb, as the title of Rabbi David Cooper's book suggests, we are closer to experiencing the organic and flowing nature of Divinity.

On my personal spiritual odyssey, the most inspiring and exciting statement in the biblical text is the naming of Divinity as *ehyeh asher ehyeh*. This very strange and magical way of Divinity naming Itself relates to the unpronounceable name YHVH, the specific proper name of Israel's God. It relates to the verb "to be" and can be translated as "I am that I am," "I am whom I am" or "I shall be that I shall be." What an incredible, mysterious and thoroughly marvelous name that grows in brilliance the more we think about it.

Divinity smiles down, I am sure, on Rabbi Mark Sameth's offering of a novel reading of the mysterious, Ineffable name that is most intriguing. In a recent article, Rabbi Sameth suggests that the reason the YHVH is unpronounceable is that the letters are reversed —

Hay Vov Hay Yud can be vocalized as the sound equivalents of the Hebrew pronouns *hu* and *hi* which are rendered in English as he and she. Combining them together, HVHY becomes becomes He-She. *Reform Judaism*

This implies that all humanity is created in the image of the Divine. The reversal of the letters adds to the magic of this sacred text and engages the readers in a very conscious way of dealing with the words.

Words confound us — the act of naming, by the nature of words themselves, is limiting. In naming Divinity, we use words that inevitably constrict The Limitless Source of Being. "I shall be that I shall be" is the most limitless type of name imaginable. God is revealed as constantly present and continually changing. Divinity as an unfolding and evolving Presence holds great potential for the new millennium. Addressing and describing Divinity in this way, we acknowledge that as we evolve, our understanding of Divinity evolves. The Divine Presence is continually in the process of opening to us, small increments at a time. As we mature, we too grow, and change in the image of this evolving creative force. Such an understanding complements Brian Swimme's description of an ever-expanding Universe that is in process.

Naming Divinity in this fashion, we bypass the misery that has been wrought over the millennia by the singular concept of a male god, in whose image one half of the human family claim to have been created. A genderless, creative and unfolding Divinity emerges not only as luminous, inspiring and numinous in the present era, but also fits with the quantum mechanical model of a multiplicity of possibilities, both for Divinity and for us.

With this as a seed concept gleaned from the Exodus text, it may be easier to go back to the historical tone of much of the Bible and read it for what it was. With this comes the insight that as we have evolved, so has our need for a different set of rules and connections, and certainly for an image of Divinity that is closer to The Creative Source of the Universe with whom we commune in our prayers and meditations.

There is another way of wrestling with this magical name for Divinity. In Judaism we are told that God asked the angels where the divinity of humankind should be placed. One of the angels, with temerity, suggested it should be placed within them, as that would be the last place that human beings would look for it.

On the journey to awakening consciousness, we become aware of the "I am," that presence of being that resides within, the seed-connection to the Divine of whom we are all a part. It is hidden, subsumed by an "alter-ego" that Eckhart Tolle, author of *A New Earth*, defines as the "egoic mind" — the incessant and ongoing stream of thought that keeps us from living in the eternal now by filling awareness with memories of the past or longings for the future.

If we struggle to understand the ultimate Jewish *koan* describing Divinity as "I am that I am," we sense a Oneness, a wholeness that is God. Silencing the "egoic mind," in meditation or by being present in the now, we drift into the peacefulness that is our inner essence. The paradox of living in human form is to find a place of balance between the "me"—the "egoic mind" that we need to navigate us through our physical lives, and the "I am" — our essence that is our connection to the spiritual realm.

For so many of us, our spiritual and religious lives are not the same. Within Reform Judaism the constant revisions of the prayer books introduce language and ideas that cause me to believe there are many within our family of families who feel this way. The revisions are refreshing, organic, and open.

Unlike those who see the Bible as written by God, I feel the inspiration for the texts was Divine but the perspiration—the work of the writing — was human. Instead of accepting the entire biblical text as sacred, I need to winnow out the history of the early Israelites as a political and historical tale. It is only in this way, with perspective, that I can understand the agenda of the priesthood in its efforts to forge a new people in covenant with Divinity. As an agenda, it was of a temporal and exclusivist nature. It no longer fits the inclusivist needs of the day; nor will such an interpretation facilitate the healing of the world.

Judaism teaches that we are in a covenantal relationship with Divinity. In his inspiring book *Minyan*, Rabbi Rami Shapiro suggests that we consider our relationship with Divinity in terms of the ten "vows" to which we commit ourselves internally, rather than thinking of them as the ten "commandments" which are given to us externally. Reading his translation of the Ten Commandments as the Ten Vows is a must for every contemporary student on a spiritual odyssey.

However we interpret the covenant, through it we understand our imperative to behave in a Godly manner for the betterment of the natural world, ourselves, and our fellow human beings. Injunctions in the text that have a chauvinist feel, from my perspective, belong in an historical context that has outlived its usefulness. In this way, the notions of a judgmental evaluation of different people, or the hierarchical separation of women from men, I understand to come from the priests rather than from Divinity. Doing otherwise does great disservice to our image of God; it can lead to the concept of a "chosen" people instead of a "choosing" people — again, in this case, a verb may be more appropriate.

Choosing to be in covenant with Divinity, we take on the responsibilities of *tikkun olam* in order to assist in the completion of the Divine plan. Again we see a theme of the continuous unfolding design of the world we inhabit. We are the agents of completion of the universe. An open awareness and a raised consciousness are the tools we require for the task with which we are blessed. The old idea of being chosen rather than choosing feeds into the "either/or" paradigm that leads to the painful feelings of the excluded, and history shows us time and again where such feelings lead.

As a calligraphic artist, I appreciate, perhaps more than many, the labor of love that goes into the writing of the scrolls. We know that today no scribal error is permitted in the texts, still lovingly written on parchment by hand. Should an error occur, the faulted leaf is not included in the scroll, but is replaced with a perfect copy. We have no way of knowing for sure that no scribal error ever occurred in the earliest of scrolls. To the contrary, Brettler informs us that the Bible, in its earliest stages, was changed as it was being written. The Dead Sea scrolls show that even in antiquity, differing versions of the same texts were available. He suggests that this is common in all classical texts.

What exactly is the Bible then? A perfect document from Divinity that came to us through Moses? An anthology of different literary forms from different authors that still inspire and puzzle us today? I see biblical study as a rewarding and ongoing challenge to approach the text with an open mind, searching for the poetry that inspires, and the themes that remain relevant to the creation of an egalitarian society as compared to the historical elements related to the past, on the spiral of time.

The mystery, the intimate relationship between the stories, the readers, and the writers, is the very foundation of the unfolding aspect of an evolving humanity, and the name *eheyeh asher eheyeh* may be the key to unlocking yet another layer, perhaps Torah's greatest gift to us.

And The Sacred Feminine? As an intimate aspect of Divinity Itself, like the name, the texts, the layers of meaning that elusively appear and then vanish as others are found, She is constantly present and continually changing — the ultimate and eternal Shape-shifter. Within a patriarchal system, attempts were made to subsume Her image into the Oneness of Divinity that language, society, and culture have understood as exclusively masculine. Created in Her image, women have remembered Her, and dancing in Eve's footsteps, will continue to call up the memory that is locked within the intuitive side of men, until all are able to release the grip on our present "either/or" paradigm and welcome in the "both/and" partnership mode of being which is unfolding.

Part Three: Feeling

The Sacred Feminine Revisited

Minds filled with compassion hear no negativity.
From Buddhist wisdom

Right-brained reminiscences

The Dreamer within is familiar with a sense of longing — for connection, for meaning, and for transformation. We sense a deep impulse of wanting that drives us to fully develop the unique talents with which we were blessed to make a difference in our lives, leaving the world a little better because we were present in it. We long for this transformation for ourselves, and in the process, our world. We long for meaningful relationships with family and friends, community, the Earth, and Divinity Itself. We yearn for an image of God that is inclusive.

Deep connection brings satisfaction and joy. As emotional beings, we experience many different emotions and feelings in the course of a single day. Emotions are physiological reactions to the world around us as we perceive it — a range of subjective feelings which, unlike the term "emotion" may be easier to define. Tolle reminds us that instinctive responses to threat — anger, fear and pleasure are the primordial forms of emotion. The body's response is filtered through our thoughts — these responses are emotions. The body cannot tell the difference between the actual situation and the thought; it will react in the same way for both. Emotions, Tolle states, like other facets of our human experience operate as dualities. They dwell in *Chronos*. States of being on the other hand, that emanate from within rather than as a response to an external event or thought — love, peace and joy are aspects of our being, facets of *Kairos*. As such they have no opposite.

Feelings come in varying kinds and degrees. The range is broad and from a zone of the "feel-good" sensations (unconditional love, joy, hope, and peace) we can shift into the borderland of surprise. We can move from contentment and acceptance to what we consider the uncomfortable feelings — annoyance, irritation, anger, despair, diminishment, guilt, and disgust.

Much of our time is spent in adding value judgments to our feelings that would encourage us to seek only that which makes us feel good and avoid situations that don't. Tolle reminds us that when we add thought and judgment to feelings, we shift from present to past or future. This shift moves us into "egoic mind" and opens up the possibility of varying degrees of discomfort. As we mature we realize that the feelings we consider negative and the challenging experiences we all endure come as great personal teachers. They motivate movement or expand our understanding of ourselves and our place in the universe. We don't consciously look for such experiences but ultimately can learn to be grateful for the resultant growth that transforms us. Change is often only sought when discomfort demands something different.

As we mature, we learn to trust our "gut feelings" when we intuit a disconnect between what we feel and the information we gather superficially through our normative five senses. Experience verifies that our intuitive sense works instantly and accurately and we learn to trust the more substantive knowledge that we glean in this fashion. How does this apply to our "feelings" about the God we come to know through our religious training? What do we do when we sense a divide between our thoughts and feelings in this most important aspect of our lives? Do we trust our feelings? Reconnecting with the Sacred Feminine brings a sense of joy — an ancient remembering of truths long known, then forgotten and now recalled.

What feelings do we have about our religious traditions? Hopefully they encourage us to bring healing to this world and to foster peaceful and affirming relationships between ourselves and those with whom we are connected.

The question of the existence of the Sacred Feminine in Judaism stirs up many different emotions and feelings. Does such a concept tear at the fabric of Judaism that has survived for thousands of years? As the emerging feminist energies awaken feelings of anger at the disenfranchisement, alienation, and marginalization of women in patriarchal settings, many look for a change that will bring a more inclusive religious and spiritual framework, welcoming women and men alike.

The writings of the earlier Jewish feminist scholars — Susannah Heschel, Rabbi Lynn Gottlieb, and Judith Plaskow to name just a few, remind us that since the 1970s, we have made progress. Within liberal Jewish communities, women rabbis, cantors, and educators are no longer rare exceptions. Women rabbis represent almost half of those being ordained in the Reform Movement today. We are in the midst of a perceptible transformation and now are accustomed to seeing women leading services, teaching Torah, conducting and creating life-cycle ceremonies in both traditional and new ways.

Today women throughout the world celebrate a feminist or women's *seder* at Passover in addition to the traditional one. Many include an orange on a ceremonial *seder* plate. Urban legend has modified the story behind this custom. In the 1980s Susannah Heschel included an orange on her *seder* plate in protest of the exclusion of gays and lesbians from the general Jewish community. I do so each year because of the urban legend I had read that Heschel, when leading a prayer service was told that she had as much right to be doing so as an orange has a place on a *seder* plate. The theme of both versions of the story has the same effect. It remains a wonderful symbol to remind us of the restrictions that still bind some of us at a time when we celebrate liberation.

Some of the new creative energy in the spiritual lives of Jewish women is seen in the popularity of constantly evolving celebrations. A *Rosh Chodesh* (New Moon) gathering is now observed by many — each group developing personal styles and themes. Penina Adelman's book, *Miriam's Well* is an inspirational resource. Additionally, celebrations should mark the milestones in the life cycle of women — from community welcoming and naming ceremonies for baby girls, to the creation of rituals to mark the onset and completion of the menstrual cycle, or to mourn miscarriage and still-births. Rainbows of color brighten Reform Temples each week as many women now choose to wear a colorful *tallit* (prayer shawl) and *kippar* (head covering) during worship.

Changes are evident too within the worship services and Torah study that is conducted weekly. Refreshing transformation in our prayer books now names Divinity with gender-free labels. Women are interested in creating *midrashim* that fill in the many gaps in the Bible about the women. Once we become aware, these omissions glare back at us from the text. Anita Diamant's book, *The Red Tent*, a *midrash* about our foremothers, enjoyed an overwhelming success within both Jewish and general circles. Initial anger at the injustice of marginalizing women based on a fixed and literal understanding of the text was, and remains, a perfect spark to discomfort us, reawakening and stirring our passions, making us aware of things we may not have previously noticed. With awareness comes change and with change, anger softens and we learn to move forward.

No longer in the ghetto, Jewish communities in America enjoy the opportunity of seeing and sampling what other spiritual traditions have to offer. Because Judaism has adapted, it has survived for thousands of years in the many places into which is has been cast by the diaspora. Many different regional traditions and practices add to a constantly evolving Jewish framework. Self-assured in the knowledge and appreciation of what their own tradition offers, Jews can explore other teachings and incorporate what they find meaningful and soulful — often finding, with surprise, that similar teachings exist within Judaism if they had only known the right questions to ask.

American Jewish romance with Eastern religions in general and Buddhism in particular is an example. Searching for a practice to turn inwards, many Jews have found a practice within Buddhism which complements their roots. Often, to their surprise, they rediscover Jewish meditation practices that were present but never taught. With a new awareness of what was missing from their spiritual lives, many revisit their own tradition, conscious and comfortable. Meditation certainly belongs in both faith communities.

Buddhism teaches that attachment is the cause of our suffering. It encourages an attitude of detachment-to-outcome as a basis for equilibrium. Judaism however, honors the feelings of discontent arising from desire and attachment, seeing in longing, the beginning of movement and separation from the status quo to a more fulfilling possibility.

The ongoing brutal oppression of the Burmese Buddhists makes one wonder how such cruelty will be ever be halted if the people are not able to rise up — politically and/or spiritually. At the same time, in a climate of deprivation, oppression and stark fear, people are learning the skills of spiritual fortitude, strength, and compassion. Is one more important for spiritual growth than another?

Thankfully most people do not have to face such extreme horror. Instead most deal with longing and desire in a comparatively benign environment. We learn that longing for "things" in our consumerist society never brings contentment — we are bombarded with new and novel items we had not even thought about and then believe we have to have. As a result of our awakening ecological consciousness, we are starting to examine the wastefulness of this harmful American practice and beginning to realize that such accumulation is destroying our planet while leaving us with a gnawing emptiness within. This is not the only form of yearning that we experience. The longing for meaning is not fulfilled with material objects which are always temporary in nature. Longing for a better, more egalitarian, ethical and just culture motivates humanity to seek social change for the betterment of all.

While Judaism has never discouraged its practitioners from enjoying the material "stuff" of this world, it teaches the concomitant sense of responsibility that accompanies the accumulation of wealth. As custodians of all that we possess, the more resources we enjoy, the greater the need for us to give back to society in appreciation of our good fortune.

Desire and longing — initiators of change, or feelings from which we should detach? Which is the most compelling of these apparently opposing views? As with most paradoxical concepts, balance will be found as a midpoint somewhere between these two truths of attaching or detaching emotion to our innate sense of desire. Longing for a more inclusive spiritual wisdom is what motivates a critical examination of the basic tenets and teachings of a faith tradition that holds the possibility of new interpretation. Presented here is the image of an evolving Divinity named "I shall be that I shall be," and a religious response to life that must evolve and grow, informed by thoughts and feelings about ourselves and the present. Without longing, without an attachment to the possibility of something more, the status quo remains intact and the natural tendency towards change and growth is stultified.

There are multiple levels of perceiving and processing reality and our places in it. Just as a flower is not aware of the point of beginning and ending of its petals and stem in relationship to one another, trying to separate our thinking and emotional lives is contrived at best. Thoughts and feelings flow together, often seamlessly, just as insight from the realm of intuition helps shape and co-join what we think and feel; in combination, input from all levels influence the actions we take.

In the twenty-first century what is frightening about the Sacred Feminine? Women are awakening from the deep sleep of alienation imposed on them in societies that worship Divinity-made-male. Jews tried to distinguish themselves from the surrounding cultures in the Ancient Near East. No longer living in the midst of goddess-worshipping cultures, is it necessary to mindlessly fear such approaches to Divinity?

Remembering that how we name and image God tell us, first and foremost, about ourselves, what do we aspire to become? Labels do not alter the essence of The Source of All Life that is beyond gender. The Sacred Feminine exemplifies an inspirational archetype or patterning that encourages women to become all that they can be. The characteristics of this role model become the clarion call to develop feminine attributes to their most creative and powerful levels. Women learn to love unconditionally and become fully present for those, including themselves, who need attention. They honor the expression of righteous anger in the face of injustice, in productive ways that will bring change. The awakening Sacred Feminine also reminds them to pay attention and honor their intuitive sense which offers a complementary knowledge to that which is learned through the intellect.

The Sacred Feminine encourages us to acknowledge our own need for autonomy and authenticity in our experiences as women, who, as nurturers and caregivers exercise the maternal instinct in diverse ways. The ultimate nature of mothering is the ability to unconditionally love the child with comfort, care and nurture, necessary for the development of security and self-esteem; similarly, when at our most vulnerable — in need and in pain, we yearn for the same reassurance through our connection to God. Prayer, however, is more than supplication — in moments of gratitude we wish to express and share our appreciation with a God that is close enough for conversation; in moments of stillness, we want a sense of connection.

The immanent, caring, and nurturing aspect of God is something we sense through our feelings rather than our thoughts. Most women would probably describe this as the feminine face of Divinity, the source of our connectedness to all human beings as well as the animal and plant kingdoms of the Earth that nourish us. At the same time, we look for a source of strength when we need to stand firm in adversity as we face challenges seemingly too big for us to handle. Such images can be found in the ferocious anger that a mother displays when her children are at risk.

We want connection and relationship with Something or Someone beyond ourselves who knows us completely and loves us still, who will deeply listen and soothe our troubled spirits, who will gently smile away the seemingly insurmountable obstacles we see blocking our way, and who will inspire us with wisdom to overcome any difficulty. In traditional Jewish belief, all these qualities are included in the Oneness of God — perhaps, for some who search, seemingly too well concealed in the transcendent male God.

As we look at our world out of balance, where we see Nature being destroyed and humanity locked in a prison of misunderstanding, we sense the tangible effects of the loss of the Sacred Feminine in our lives. The Dreamer within longs for Her reappearance as a role model as we seek to re-balance our world. The Dreamer too, reminds us that in harmony we can come together and cry each other's tears, acknowledging that humanity is a single family, however diverse its members.

Jewish Women and the Goddess

As a remnant of the Sacred Feminine, the elusive figure of the *Shechinah* is now being reclaimed and reintroduced in contemporary prayer. This term is presently recognized beyond the borders of the Jewish community, and is used in diverse women's spirituality groups. According to the author Raphael Patai, the word "*Shechinah*" is talmudic rather than biblical, referring to the perceivable presence of Divinity on Earth — the ephemeral trace of The Ineffable that we may be privileged to see or hear. In biblical times, it was believed that God, like the other sky gods of the peoples of the Ancient Near East, dwelled in the clouds. The tabernacle, or *mishkan* was constructed to house this Presence who descended to Earth from time to time. The word itself comes from the Hebrew word *shachan* meaning to dwell or settle.

The image evolved in the *midrashic* literature into an independent feminine divinity who, through her identification with and compassion for humanity, will forever stand in its defense before The Holy One. Is the *Shechinah* the Jewish symbol that fulfills the same mythic and metaphoric purpose as Mary in Roman Catholicism? Are these the aspects of the Sacred Feminine that we remember, and have kept alive in our hearts and souls?

In the late biblical period we find the development of the concept of angels — intermediaries who for some were believed to be created by God; for others, they are seen to be part or aspects of The Oneness Itself. These beings/aspects could mediate between Divinity and humanity. Rather than being seen as a separate female divinity in a monotheistic religion, we see in Judaism the perceptible, immanent aspect of God referred to as the *Shechinah*, and understood to be the feminine face of The Holy One.

Also understood as a feminine manifestation was *Hochmah* or wisdom, believed to have been the first creation of Divinity, the one that eventually became described as "God's wife." Hebrew is a language that uses male and female forms for words and so *Shechinah*, like *Hochmah*, both use the feminine suffix '-ah'. Whether the language then is responsible for the identification of these two concepts as feminine, or whether the concept developed in association and response to a deep need and memory within the people at that time, is hard to say. The idea of feminine divinities was common in our earlier untold history and surrounding cultures of the time.

For many women, the idea of being protected and held beneath the wings of the *Shechinah* is very appealing and carries the concept of sanctuary as the following personal incident indicates. I no longer recall whether the image I first experienced many years ago at a time of vulnerability came in a daydream or during sleep. Neither do I remember the details of the emotional turmoil of that moment, but this image has remained clear and constant over the years. The ephemeral Presence I experienced was immense and definitely feminine. I saw myself seated beside what I assumed was the left knee of an enormous, seated, ethereal, and ancient figure who appeared to be swathed in white mist. I saw no physical features — but the image was one of an overwhelming Presence of unconditional love. In contact with this energy I felt totally protected, soothed and whole. I could sense a caring and gentle amusement at my feelings of the moment in which my situation seemed to be real — and serious. Now, years later, as a grandmother, I recognize this quality in myself as I am called to soothe the hurts of my grandchild. Whatever causes his temporary discomfort seems to him to be of enormous significance. I find myself smiling at the seriousness with which he perceives the situation. Now each time I meditate or imagine a place of comfort, this same powerful image opens up as if for the first time. For me, it was a *Kairos* experience of the energy of the Sacred Feminine.

Women find comfort in the idea of the *Shechinah* as an Earth-bound traveler, dwelling among us during the exile of our physical lives on our human journey. She feels our pains and comforts us in times of sorrow. It is a beautiful and nurturing image and gives us a sense of closeness to the Source of Life who brings universes into being.

As we follow the development of the concept of the separation of Divinity from humanity, the idea of a love relationship becomes one that is parental — the people Israel choose the covenantal contract of love that binds them to God. The Sacred Feminine thus moves deeper into a state of concealment. Evidence of this can be seen in many biblical and prophetic statements, and may best be exemplified in the biblical Song of Songs, which is read as a love story between God and Jewish people.

In the course of the development of monotheism, the concept of the Sacred Feminine evolved in interesting ways. Instead of describing any form of feminine divinity, sanctity is connected with certain aspects of religious life and practice that become the bridge to Divinity. Such feminine concepts are the Sabbath Bride who is welcomed each week at sunset on Friday — she remains until the appearance of the first stars on Saturday. God is described in this context as the Bridegroom. Is the strong association of the Sabbath and the Sacred Feminine the reason that women, representative of this energy, were the ones to light the *Shabbat* candles each week?

Additionally when a married couple make love on Friday night — on the Sabbath, it is considered to be a *mitzvah* and a bridge connecting the couple to Divinity. The spirit of the *Shechinah* is believed to be present with the couple engaged in sacred sexuality which in turn was believed to hasten the reunification of The *Shechinah* with the Holy One.

In his book, *The Hebrew Goddess*, Patai draws attention to the *Bat Kol*, the feminine voice of Divinity "through whom God's will was made audible on earth." Is this reminiscent of the other oracles, such as at Delphi? Additionally, feminine images are associated with the Torah itself, and the Earth (*adamah*).

Patai's work leads us to believe that contrary to what we may have thought, the concealed Sacred Feminine exists in the Jewish God-concept, and depending on the belief and practice of the Jews, She reveals or conceals Herself. Patai furthers states that the open attitude of Jews to sexuality as wholesome and sacred is connected to the imagery of the Divine Groom and his Bride. Kabbalists even described the approach of the sun and the moon during an eclipse in sexual terms. The association of women and the moon became an important part of women's rituals in Judaism with the monthly celebration of the *Rosh Chodesh* ceremony — the welcoming of the New Moon each month as we will see in the next chapter.

Judaism and Wicca

Earlier, mention was drawn to the negative knee-jerk reaction towards the words "goddess" and "pagan." To the list can be added the word "witch." With the long lens of history, Jews may come to understand the ancient priests' desire at that time to separate the developing community from its neighbors. It may have been necessary to allow the creation of a new and different way of life in the midst of others. Priestly disdain passed success-fully down through the generations, as they hoped it would. What purpose does it now serve? Does a religious life require us to remain in fear of what others believe or do?

Looking at the tenets of the pagan traditions today in which the Sacred Feminine is revealed and accessible, one sees an Earth-centered belief system that identifies with the wonder and majesty of Nature and her cycles. Wiccans are encouraged to love all others and are commanded to do no harm. There is a sense of the sacred that permeates everything. The image of Divinity worshipped as Goddess in her different aspects is no different, other than gender, from either the patriarchal labels we use today, "God, Lord, Father, and King" or the gender-free labels of "Fountain, Rock and Source" that hearken back to our own sense of awe in the presence of Nature. Just as the latter names for Divinity refer to different aspects of a single God, the same may be said of polytheistic communities who attach different aspects of the natural world to their image and naming of Divinity. Within Wiccan circles, there is much freedom of individual expression and practice and the encouragement to question everything.

How different is the pagan celebration of the natural, seasonal cycle of time from many of our own traditional festivals, which now connect with historical events, and were originally seasonal and tied to a lunar calendar?

Chanukkah, our festival of light, celebrated in remembrance of the miracle of light and associated with the story of the

Maccabees, remains the ancient celebration of light in the winter darkness in the northern hemisphere. Spring brings new growth to the trees, and the celebration of Passover now commemorates a myth of redemption in keeping with the liberation and renewal of the life-force. *Shavuot*, one of the three Nature festivals that were times of pilgrimage to ancient Jerusalem, has its roots in the joyful celebration of summer. Tradition has added the festival of receiving the Ten Commandments.

In the fall, Judaism's original main *Chag* (festival) was that of *Sukkot* (booths/temporary shelters) rather than *Rosh Hashanah* and *Yom Kippur*. *Sukkot* offers an invitation to dwell out in Nature for a week to acknowledge the transitory quality of life. In the northern hemisphere, this festival acknowledges that the natural world prepares for the wane of creative energies as the darkness of the lengthening nights approach. *Tu B'shvat* in late winter heralds the new growth that approaches.

In the southern hemisphere, all festivals are celebrated on the same dates but occur during opposite seasons. Such celebration is affected by the place in which people find themselves. Just as Christian friends in South Africa struggled to recreate snow-covered trees in the heat of the summer as they prepared for Christmas (some resorting to aloes sprayed with white powder) *Chanukkah*, a minor holiday, lost its significance in the enjoyment of the summer sunshine and vacation cycle. In the United States, subject as all are to the massive marketing machine of commerce, *Chanukkah* has been elevated to a festival of major importance. Rather than the gift-giving it has generated, Jews can revel in the fact that they too have a celebration of light in the midst of winter darkness, even if this primal celebration is concealed under the remembrance of an historical event.

Pagan belief honors the grandeur of Nature as Judaism does. It stresses ecological concern as does Judaism. Wiccans pray to and image Divinity as feminine in form. Jews are free to choose masculine, feminine or non-gendered images and names for The

Eternal One. As we look at our lives as women and reclaim our places, authentic and valued because of who we are, we open to the awakening Sacred Feminine. We can lift western religion's veil of fear with which she was shrouded and buried in the dark and watery grave of the unconscious. Once brought to light, as with all Shadow figures, we recognize that we have nothing to fear from Her.

Lilith: Shadow of *The Shechinah*?

The legends of Lilith show us, in mythic terms, the intended fate of the Sacred Feminine in patriarchal Judaism if she was to be an inspiration for women's sense of strength and autonomy. Lilith was the legendary first wife of Adam who took flight rather than submit to her husband. Her image was demonized. She became evil incarnate, a threat to men and women alike, particularly to women in labor! Like the reclamation of The *Shechinah* as the feminine face of Divinity, modern women are reclaiming Lilith, acknowledging her symbolic independence as our own, as we remove the dusty, worn and terror-laden robes with which she was clothed for centuries. Subordination and marginalization deny self-fulfillment as they alienate. Re-visioning Lilith as a positive stereotype encourages feminine empowerment. With strength and confidence rather than fear, we can afford to look and learn from our pagan sisters who probably represent most closely a form of religious life that existed before the patriarchy.

The author Starhawk is a noted authority in the American pagan movement. She is a Jewish witch who wants to reclaim the original meaning of the word "witch" as an honored term. At a Jewish women's one-day retreat in San Francisco several years ago, she gave a talk entitled, "What is a nice Jewish girl like you doing in a coven like this?" Listening to her words those of us present came to the realization that the values by which women like Starhawk live are familiar to us.

The transition from wise-woman to witch occurred in historic times as the church wished for men to claim the feminine abilities and inclinations of healing and counsel. Terms like "witch," "hag," and "crone" were all once terms of respect for the older woman that have been mercilessly sullied. Wiccan practitioners wish to reclaim those honored titles. Wicca poses no threat to Judaism once one moves away from the limiting and historically-laden world of semantics and linguistics. Starhawk's belief translates into action and sacred service as exemplified in her protest at the opening of the Diablo Canyon nuclear power plant close to where I now live. As an aside, "Devil's" Canyon is a fascinating name/place for a power plant!

Separation from, and fear of, others in any religious sense may be an emotion of the past that can be replaced with equilibrium as one looks, listens and learns. In this way all of us can begin to celebrate the diversity around us and find harmonious ways to share our differences, as we respectfully create a pluralistic society.

Feminist Re-visioning

Jewish feminists find ourselves in a dilemma. With a definitely patriarchal tone to the texts upon which our faith is based, what do we do? Reject the text and move away from our traditional faith? Ignore what now glares back at us with every reading of the scrolls? Reinterpret in a way that now not only allows us to remain part of our community but opens the ancient words in new and fascinating ways to men and women around us?

There are passages in the text that are problematic, minimalizing women and their authentic female experiences. Women were placed in proscribed roles, relegated to the environs of the home, and denied authentic self-determination. From my perspective, putting statements of a discriminatory nature in the mouth of God, as the reason to perpetrate such social structuring demeans the nature of Divinity.

I have always been much less drawn to *Halachah* (the legalistic interpretation of the *Tanach*) and more interested in the philosophy and theology of Judaism. The *halachic* stance is the respected opinion of men wrestling over the ages with a text that remains pertinent. Nothing more, nothing less. Once awakened, women do not feel the need to blindly follow tradition because past generations have done so. Many see historic Judaism as an incomplete approach to life because the input of one-half of the community is absent.

Those fortunate enough not to have not been personally and negatively impacted by this patriarchal interpretation of our faith, acknowledge the tragic results that other women, not as fortunate, have experienced over the ages. In the Reform Jewish setting in which I was raised and have remained a participant, I have never known a Judaism in which my presence or that of the women around me, even those of my mother's generation, was not considered a valid part of the community. I sang in the Temple choir as a child, standing at the side of the *bimah* (pulpit) in full view of the Congregation. I was never relegated to an upstairs balcony or a divided Temple setting where men and women sat in separate sections. I grew up seeing other women on the *bimah* accepting *aliyot* (the honor of going up to bless the reading of the Torah). I celebrated my *Bat Mitzvah* at age thirteen by reading from the opening verses of Genesis. Women were active on the Temple Boards. None of the women I knew personally had to feel humiliated by trying to obtain a *get* — a Jewish divorce issued by an all male *Beth Din* (Hebrew for a Religious Court). All of this occurred in South Africa before the advent of women rabbis or cantors; even more remarkable perhaps in a society that seemed to trail the United States by at least a decade or two in so many areas of life.

I clearly remember, however, a brush with this attitude and practice in my twenties and can easily recall my own distaste and amazement. Still living in South Africa at the time, I went to the home of friends who were orthodox Jews. They were in mourning, and I wanted to participate in the prayer service after the funeral of my friend's father — expecting that I would be welcomed as I would have been in a Reform home. I was invited to join the other women in the kitchen as the prayer service was about to begin in the living room. Long before my feminist self had started to awaken (or so I used to think) I was shocked that I was not welcome at the prayer service itself. I wished my friend well and left before the service started.

Perpetuating the imbalance

Any woman not afforded the right to be an authentic, fully participating member of the community at a level of her choosing bears the burden of injustice. She exists somewhat invisibly on the periphery; she knows firsthand the feel of inequality and the inability to contribute to the wealth of knowledge regarding the experience of the community.

Women may be able to accept the patriarchal tone of the text as a historic account of a period in our immature history — even see the attempt to improve the position for women in the community as compared to that of women in surrounding patriarchal cultures at the time; however, we balk at these texts being understood as a God-given directive to maintain a status quo. Women want to stop the continuation of an inequitable approach to Divinity, society, and life.

Women can be most effective in changing the patriarchal system once we let go of the initial anger we feel when first confronting the injustices in this paradigm. In a patriarchal system, diminishment is not reserved only for women and those men who are relegated to lower rungs on the ladder maintained by the white anglo-saxon heterosexual males. Those at the top, distanced from their own feminine energies in order to maintain the status quo, function in a diminished way too — out of touch with their feelings.

One of the most wonderful aspects of Reform Jewish practice

is the belief in a direct connection to Divinity; no-one requires the acceptance of any *Beth Din* to award or remove our Jewish badges of connection. It would seem that in voicing our contemporary views of ourselves as Jewish women, reviewing and re-visioning the texts, we retain a valid and authentic place in our Jewish communities. As we reformulate our roles and our stance, we assist other women to rethink their own positions. Some have sadly discarded their Jewish identities, feeling they could not remain within a sexist tradition; others feel alone, abandoned, and unaware that many women feel as they do, dealing with their own misgivings.

In turn, as equals within the Jewish community, we re-evaluate what we are handing down to future generations. It is possible to recreate ourselves in an egalitarian fashion. The participation of women rabbis and scholars at the discussion table at the start of the twenty first century provides a worthwhile example of how this occurs. As women reviewing our faith and traditions, we are all offered a fresh and creative impetus to add to our religious lives. Our challenge is more than just to find equal footing in a tradition that discriminates in any way against half of its community; rather it is to recreate a Judaism that encourages and welcomes the full participation of everyone. Many Jewish men feel the same way and are assisting in the effort.

We may all know success when our religious and spiritual lives are one. For too many, it seems, the two are disparate. Many spiritually awakened women feel, if forced to choose, spirituality would trump religion. How then do we start to bring the two into harmony? We need first to examine the texts, on which all is based, with new eyes. We need to feel comfortable as we read between the lines and ask questions — even those to which there may not be any answers. Who were the women, with their own thoughts, feelings, and aspirations, named and unnamed, within the texts?

That, however, is not where the questioning must end. We need to look at the authorship of the Bible. Just as we best understand the contemporary books we read today when we know something about the authors, the same applies to our sacred literature. We are troubled today with individuals who proclaim to know what God wants from us. Why then are we afraid to look at the role of the priests in our tradition and carefully examine their words as coming from a human and politicized source, rather than accepting the validity of their self-acclaimed role in speaking for God?

The ever-growing library of the thoughts of feminist scholars is shining new light on the ancient texts. Many Jewish women in the early stages of the feminist movement struggled because others saw the Bible as the progenitor of the patriarchy. Such criticism came from those who neither knew the patriarchy had been established long before the writing of the texts, nor that the scribes were living within the limitations of the "either/or" paradigm that the patriarchy developed. The written record in the Bible is an early literary insight into the opinions prevalent during the earlier patriarchal times.

How does this impinge on the concept of Divinity? Hebrew, a language with feminine and masculine forms can be said to have gendered God. The use of male nouns and pronouns linguistically birthing the image of God as male is just a start. The patriarchal mindset of the time, imaged God not only as male but in hierarchical terms that stratify, separating Divinity from humanity as the Master and King who is separated and removed from his servants. It is much more than just the use of male nouns and pronouns for Divinity that is problematic. With the hierarchical image of Master/servant, we seem to be at odds with the concept of being in partnership with Divinity as we attempt to fulfill our role in *tikkun olam*. Is the recognition and implementation of the partnership model what is necessary for healing of society?

Operating in a "both/and" paradigm that an egalitarian approach bids us to do, we know there are more possibilities than either being subservient to the Divine or being equal. If we see ourselves as part of the Divine whole — cells in the organs of consciousness in the Divine Being, as suggested by Rabbi Lawrence Kushner, we can comprehend that we each have worth and magnificence, while at the same time knowing that no one of us is God.

Each one of us is a unique individual, totally unlike anyone else. At the same time, we are sparks of godliness, identical to all other cells of consciousness that make up the Divine Being. We each have an individual and unique piece of the puzzle, a vital link necessary for the completion of the whole.

Just as we need Divinity, Divinity needs us in order to experience the emotional world of materiality. Placing discriminatory and hierarchical sentiments into the mouth of the Divine, as the androcentric Priestly source does, discredits our image of ourselves, and more profoundly, gives us great pause to consider the nature of Divinity.

Surely the most significant information we can glean from the fundamentals of any religious tradition is what it teaches about the nature of God. Without any idea of the nature of Divinity in whose image we are created, how can we claim to understand who we are, why we are here, and where we are going? There are as many ways of interpreting this concept as there are readers of the text. In living our lives creatively, and learning to use our free will responsively in the choices we make, we align with the Divine template. We open ourselves to all the possibilities and potentials of that Divine spark of creativity that resides within us. As women, we want to find Divinity within the sacred texts encouraging our participation in a relationship in which we do not feel "other." A non-gendered image helps us break away from hierarchy.

There are attitudes expressed in the text, so sexist in tone that egalitarian scholars need to challenge them. The attitude towards purity and the menstrual cycle, responsible for the mysterious ability to birth a new generation, is an example. To view and label this natural and miraculous process as being "unclean/impure" is offensive for those who stand in awe of the entire creative process. The notion of going to a *mikveh* (ritual bath) after periods of "impurity" is something many find archaic; the concept of the "impurity" of a woman after giving birth to a child is startling — made even worse when we are told that the so-called impurity lasts for seven days after giving birth to a boy, and fourteen days after birthing a baby girl! Where is the touch of Divinity in such a concept?

Examples of this nature can be seen as the actions of a patriarchal priesthood stratifying the community, favoring the male half of humanity as being in the image of a male god. Their subsequent status becomes elevated. It denigrates women for the singular and holy ability to birth future generations. Just as we question the connection to holiness of the modern self-proclaimed prophets of exclusivity, we need to question a similar tone resonating from the voice of the patriarchal priest in his denigration of the physical representation of the Sacred Feminine on Earth.

The concept of separation may be seen to play out on the stage of the Jewish tradition. Dividing what is sacred from what is not, is basic to Jewish practice. *Shabbat* is made holy by separating this day from the rest of the week. Marriage is seen as a separate and sanctified relationship. Judaism as a way of life can be seen as separated from all others and its followers called to keep that separation. There is a deep shadow to dividing reality in this way.

Philosopher Martin Buber teaches that we have the choice of treating "the other" in one of two ways — I/thou or I/it. The spiritual journey asks us consider everything around us in an I/thou perspective. There is sanctity too in the secular. The division of one from the other may express the outer limits of this duality. We can see the sacred in every moment of each day and find the extraordinary in the commonplace. Every moment is laden with magical portent. Every righteous action we take can be holy. Surely the difference between the sacred and the secular lies in our perceptions and intentions. Is not the purpose of reciting blessings every day and the performing of *mitzvot* (the imperative for righteous behavior) to raise consciousness to the level of converting the secular to the status of the sacred?

Our challenge then becomes, for example, how to make Shabbat a special day among other days that have creative possibility for encountering the sacred. In the same way, marriage is a sanctified relationship of bonding and commitment within a range of family and communal relationships that are sanctified and holy.

The idea of "a chosen people" adds the suggestion of Divine blessing to separation. Such an exclusivist concept is inconsistent with a worldview of inclusivity. It is preferable to consider being one of a "choosing people" — choosing to take on the responsibilities of the covenant of *tikkun olam*.

A history of discrimination against Jews colors our feeling about separating ourselves from others in our communities. The Shadow side of this separation is the exclusivist attitude fostered in its adherents. How many Jews are willing to know more about other religious traditions, beliefs and practices? Secure in our own, it should not be a threatening experience to learn something about other people's beliefs. Our history of victimization and the inestimable damage and destruction to our people over the centuries by those of other faiths is part of our reality; however, today there are more effective and meaningful ways to protect a way of life than by isolating it — and ourselves — from the present possibilities and potential. Trying to understand the basics of other traditions gives us an insight into how others think. Welcoming others of different religious and spiritual communities into our

Temples to experience the way we worship and function — to understand something of what we believe and why — helps foster an understanding and respect for Judaism.

Whispers from the past

As we yearn for a more egalitarian future by seeking the Sacred Feminine, we can do more than merely dream. Perhaps the dream is a portal into *Kairos* — the imaginative realm in which new forms evolve. This ephemeral world of hidden and symbolic images plays an important role in the text itself. Dreams ask us to delve into the mystery and invite our attention. The Talmud reminds us that a dream unexamined is like a letter from Divinity left unopened. Our longing to be able to reconnect with our tradition in new and meaningful ways offers an opportunity to understand ourselves.

Women rabbis and scholars like author Marcia Falk are opening up more than biblical text. They are creating vibrant new prayers in English and Hebrew whose flowing imagery and language is both timely and timeless. Falk's prayers are non-hierarchical, removing the Master/server relationship of the older, traditional prayer formats. The feminist imagery is Nature-based, beautiful and poetic.

Other feminist scholars have made us aware of the many omissions in the biblical texts. We do not have the stories of the women in their own words. In many instances the actions taken by women have been critical to the story. What would we know about them if they had told their stories in their own words? Devising *midrashim* (creative stories based on biblical text) to fill in these gaps is a honored way of getting to know these women and lift their one-dimensional quality off the page and into life. Examples of two of my own *midrashim* are included in the appendix.

This practice can ameliorate our anger in creative ways. To write our own *midrashim* we start by asking questions about what is missing from the text. If the tales had been written by women for women, and were told rather than read, we would all come to know them very differently. Women respond to this form of storytelling; it taps into ancestral memories or creates alternate possibilities, past and future.

As we begin, the words of Monique Wittig are encouraging:

"There was a time . . . you say you have lost all recollection . . . remember, remember – or failing that, invent. " *Standing Again at Sinai*

Start to name the nameless women in texts and try to feel what it would be like to live their lives. Into the text we introduce the women who are missing altogether. Noah, we are told, had three sons. And what of Noah's nameless wife? Many of the women are totally ignored as the mothers of the generations listed only as sons of their fathers. Others are labeled as "wife" or "daughter" of a named man. Still others remain totally nameless like the tragic figure of the *pilegesh* (concubine?) in the Book of Judges.

We look at the named women and ask everything we do not know about them and their lives. What would Dina tell us about why she went out to seek the women of the land? Was she raped by Shechem or were they lovers? What motivated Zipporah's actions after Moses encounters an angel? What of Sarah and Hagar's relationship? Was Sarah fulfilling a part assigned her in the story of humanity by allowing Hagar's descendents to forge their own identity? Would the two sons of Abraham, who come together at his death, be fulfilling their destiny in setting up the polarities we need in order to choose to love one another? How did Sarah feel on discovering that Abraham had taken her son, her only child born so late in her life, up to Mt. Moriah where the father believed he was to bind and sacrifice Isaac?

We can turn to the texts with a new and creative vision. We

find that adding the names, voices, and stories of our foremothers to the tales, in an attempt to replace what was omitted in a text written by men for men, is a start. We become aware of how little biblical material directly deals with the lives of women. Stories are told about them rather than from them. Just as today's physicians are showing that the male model as the norm for all people is not a satisfactory model for women, how then does a male telling of the story regarding the behavior, thoughts, and feelings of women gel with what those women would have described if sharing their stories with other women?

It is interesting to observe our own reactions as we become aware of how the text deals with the female characters. We realize that we may not have even noticed the loss of attention and information that suddenly stares back at us from the parchment leaves. Like "good girls" raised in a patriarchal setting, we may have assumed that this was "just the way it was," had always been, and should so remain. Once we start to read feminist literature and commentaries on the text, we become puzzled and then angered that we have been robbed of half of our history. Later we look beyond the stories about men and women towards the effects of such notions on our perceptions and understanding of Divinity.

In many areas of our lives we discover that once we have personally become an active participant in a creative endeavor, we never see things in quite the same way again. As a teenager, I watched an Italian artist carving a cameo. He cut an exquisite female form on an oval shell by painstakingly and gently removing layers of shell to reveal the form that he alone could see before he started. After seeing the refined face emerge, as he revealed what was previously concealed, I knew that never again would I see any cameo as merely an old-fashion pendant worn by my mother's generation. Experiences like this teach us the difference between looking and seeing, just as there are differences between hearing and listening. The former ways of perceiving, looking and hearing do not engage our personal sense of awareness in the same way that seeing and listening do.

We can apply this as we recreate the women in the text. They come alive in a way they never were before and now always will be. Their archetypal form lifts them off the pages of the text as they become holographic forms, shimmering before us. Savina Teubal is a writer whose creative scholarship provides us with a great example. I "coincidently" discovered her work in the early 1990s when her book *Sarah the Priestess* was "just given" to me as a casual gift by a rabbi and friend. Having read it he wondered what I would think of it. I had not heard of Teubal or her work. Today I am so grateful for that gift and for Teubal's inspiring contribution.

Her perspective of the early matriarchs of the Bible is fascinating and as women we resonate with Teubal's ideas. Over the years, I have shared her insights with members of our weekly Torah study group when we study the books of Genesis each year as part of the ongoing annual cycle of readings. My study partners are women and men who meet to read the same stories again and again each year. We are continually amazed at how different the stories seem — not because the words have changed since the previous reading, but because each year we are different from what and who we were a year before. Each year we are intrigued with Teubal's portrayal of Sarah and Hagar. As important figures in the story, meriting several verses of biblical text, one intuits that there is far more to their relationship than is indicated by the story for men.

I was always discomforted with the petty rivalries between the women in the early Bible stories and wrote my own versions of the relationship between Rachel and Leah in my *haggadah*. As two sisters who had left their homeland, presumably their mother, and all that was familiar, would it not be more likely, or certainly just as likely, that they would have been supportive of each other and the difficulties they shared?

The outpouring of books with a feminist perspective of Judaism, its texts and its practices, is inviting the creative energies of women to the table of study. This interest crosses over religious lines. Many Christian women are looking at Christianity in the same way, as revealed in the wonderful book, *The Dance of The Dissident Daughter* by Sue Monk Kidd. In her book, *The Trouble with Islam,* Muslim author, Irshad Manji, tells of her spiritual journey in her own tradition that in many ways parallels my odyssey.

Women now are reading, questioning, and reinterpreting the texts in the same way that men have for centuries. The entrance of women scholars will help to transform Judaism and create a complete body of wisdom and knowledge that honors both male and female experience and yearning.

The excitement of this present era is to watch the emergence of an evolution in our total human experience. As we reclaim and revalue our other, older abilities of intuitive understanding, we learn that dissecting the world into pieces is only half of the picture for the maturing human being. We need now to strengthen the forces that strive to bring the separated pieces together. With equally balanced polarities, we can make choices of real meaning.

Celebrating Intrafaith Diversity

Perhaps one of the things Jews long for most may be the most challenging to achieve. What about *shalom-bayit* (peace at home)? How we can learn to treasure our different approaches to Judaism as valid responses to our faith? Is there a way for those who are fundamentalist in their interpretation of Jewish practice to find common ground with those who are more liberal? It seems impossible. Reform Jews find it easy to recognize the validity of more traditional orthodoxy as one of many ways of expressing Judaism. For anyone from a fundamentalist approach it is much more challenging — perhaps impossible to accept that there are different ways of expressing universal beliefs. If one adheres to the belief that there is only one way, the right way, the "True Way," what space is there to find common ground with other approaches? As eternal optimists, we can hold on to the hope that such coming together may be difficult but possible when we move out of the "either/or" paradigm.

In other areas, such changes are happening. Quantum theory has shown that reality does not in fact function as for centuries we believed it did. It teaches us the questions we ask determine the answers we get. As applied to the physical property of light, physicists were divided and entrenched in their belief that light was either a particle or a wave. The magical answer is that it is both, and will depend on the question we ask. Wave questions generate wave answers just as particle questions generate particle answers.

If the question affects the answer, the challenge becomes finding the right questions to ask that will lead us to recognize our commonalities. Orthodox practitioners, be they Jewish or of any other religious tradition, believe that there is only one way to be authentically part of their group. More than two thirds of the Jewish community today ascribe to more liberal approaches to our faith. We open the door to finding ways for all of us to come together, appreciating the traditional way of practice and prayer as one aspect of the Jewish experience. At the same time, we marvel and enjoy the creative new forms of interpretation, worship and practice that continue to draw us back to the spiritual guidance of the tradition that may feel empty, impersonal, old-world, and without meaning.

As the understanding of a quantum suggestion of multiple possibilities infiltrates our thinking, there must be a way for the "either/or" paradigm in the religious sphere to shift into a "both/and" setting where we can learn to appreciate each other's perspectives and the gifts they bring.

The division that exists within the Jewish community is

tragic. If after several thousand years, we still stand in judgment of each other, what have we learned? We may differ in our decisions about practice and custom, but we are ostensibly one people, sharing a history and a vision. We are all post-Holocaust Jews. In the enormity of this tragedy perpetrated against our people, as well as others deemed less than human by the Nazi regime, no distinction was made about what form of Judaism its victims practiced. This indescribable reign of terror still looms large in our contemporary consciousness and casts a giant shadow. We are still too close in time to the events of 1939-45 to really understand the enormity of what occurred when one-third of Jews, and millions of others were tortured and slaughtered. How can humanity deal with the horror of the facts? Some survivors lost all faith in God. Jews have to deal with the aftermath of this tragedy as one people, but each in their own way.

Several years ago, I realized how close to the surface are the personal memories of those years of fear, terror, suffering, and degradation for people we meet today. Leading a *Rosh Chodesh* (New Moon) celebration that occurred the same day as the commemoration of *Yom Hashoah* (Day of Remembrance of the Holocaust), I decided to lead a discussion on the Holocaust and genocide. Each woman shared her thoughts and feelings. As the group came to the end of the sharing, I asked whether one of the things we can learn from such tragedy is how to share the pain of others, because tragic holocausts have happened since and continue to happen. A woman in our group, who as a child had been in hiding during the war years, was incensed that I would even suggest such a thing. Getting more and more agitated, she started to scream that the Nazi Holocaust was not to be compared to anything else that ever occurred before or since, and that as a *rebbetzin* (rabbi's wife) I should know better. In fact, she continued, I was no better than a Nazi myself. She left in tears.

Without having experienced what she did, how could we

judge her reaction? It was a sobering experience for all present. It dramatically brought home the different and powerful ways in which people hear the words we use. It provided an emotionally charged opportunity to hear the perspective of one in great pain and honor her views, however dissimilar from our own.

She is not alone in her belief. Without trying to minimize in any way the horror of that experience, unless one can take the pain we know and use it as an empathic point of contact with which to feel the tragedy of others, an opportunity to grow is missed. The Museum of Tolerance in Los Angeles tells the story of the tragedy of the Nazi Holocaust as well as making each visitor aware of how prejudice operates everywhere and in all of our lives. The Museum offers tools to make visitors aware of how bigotry begins, and to prevent it from destroying lives.

Judaism teaches that as members of the human family, we should love our neighbor like ourselves. Is this possible? It may be a more attainable goal if the Hebrew words are translated to read that we should love our neighbors "because" they are like us. In searching for common ground to build community, respect should be paid to our similitude as well as the distinctions that make each one of us unique.

The descriptive term "Judeo-Christian . . ." should cause us to listen with care to whatever follows this phrase. On the surface, this is a term that signals a common heritage between Jews and Christians. In reality, this is a term not usually used by Jews. This phrase normally is used as an interpretation of Judaism through a Christian perspective. Care is necessary when speaking in the name of both traditions. For example, at a recent interfaith presentation for which I was a panelist, the Christian representative assumed that like all Christians, Jews are looking for ways to avoid being damned to hell in the next life — a false assumption mistakenly believed to be part of the so-called "Judeo-Christian" view because it is part of a Christian belief. Judaism teaches that our focus needs to be in this world, that we make heaven or hell where we are by the choices we make.

While there are areas both faith communities share and on which everyone can build, it would seem more credible to hear how Jews interpret their own beliefs than have them filtered through the perspective of any other group and mindset. In so doing, it is possible to find authentic commonalities shared by both traditions, releasing many misconceptions about Judaism. Both traditions teach, in their own imagery, metaphor and symbolism, about caring for the human family and the Earth, and perhaps inherent in such love, is the duality that runs from judgment to compassion.

Where do we stand on such a continuum? How willing are each of us to see the Divinity that resides within each human being, irrespective of appearance, belief, or practice? How easy is it for us to connect with one another using the sentiments of Sanskrit greeting *Namaste* — "the sacred within me greets the sacred within you?"

The blessing of being able to experience emotions and feelings is part of the great gift of life. In the hierarchical "either/or" paradigm, emotion is separated out from our penchant for reason and is seen as a "less-than" mode of experiencing reality. In the past, abilities were aligned with gender — males, the rightful practitioners of logic and rationality were considered to be of a higher level of functioning than females who were relegated to the emotional realm of feelings. Such separation not only prevented women from acquiring the educational skills that could ultimately benefit the community; it caused a disconnect in men who became alienated from the validity and expression of their own emotions and feelings. How much of this still exists today? Jung reminds us that just as the anima exists within each man, the animus exists within each woman; we each need to balance the masculine and feminine within.

The Sacred Feminine is present, although unnamed as such in Judaism, concealed within totality of the Oneness of Divinity. As each woman aligns with the Sacred Feminine and names Her, she learns to be comfortable with her individual strengths. Her head is held a little higher and she can speak out for herself and for others. This awareness comes from a remembrance of an ancient knowledge that was once known, then forgotten and now being recalled. It is life-changing and affirming — the start of the healing that women desire. This awakening is visceral and can be described as the blossoming of a dormant seed in area of the generative second chakra that begins to flower once more after a long drought. Putting women in touch with their inner strength is empowering and brings with it courage, hope and awareness of personal integrity.

Just as society attempts to mirror God in the ways of its culture, human individuals too reflect more personal descriptions of God in their own personalities. Children lucky enough to have loving parents expect a loving God. Just as we mature and see our parents differently as fallible and yet loving, supportive of us and needing our respect, how does our image of God mature?

The Holy One/Wholly One becomes accessible in new and exciting ways when we see that male and female qualities within us can be balanced and honored, in the same way we image a Oneness that is Divinity. As we wrestle with the concept of who creates whom and in whose image, a Divinity that unites these qualities within becomes a reflection of a society that can truly achieve an egalitarian stance and at the same time offer a Source of All Life that looks like us all.

A world of harmony is possible when all feel a sense of worth, validity, and participation. Just as a strong value is placed on thought and reason in Judaism, so is there a reliance on the building of community based on compassion and caring. In the reality of contemporary life, the innate sense of caring and community building encourages philanthropy to endow the providing of institutional structures that care — hospitals and schools, social service and community centers, outreach programs and those that address social justice issues.

Surely, as a creative and caring human family we can find ways to bridge the great divide between orthodox and liberal perspectives within our traditions, not by becoming alike but by appreciating the values and goals of one another. We can learn to appreciate the differences in our own communities as well those of other faith traditions. This need not cause any sense of discomfort because the goal is not to lose oneself in the embrace of the other, but rather to find ourselves, standing proud, each a member of one family in conjunction with the diversity of others to whom we give the same rights and respect we demand for ourselves, and so dwell in the shelter of one another.

Part Four: Action

The Sacred Feminine Restored

Had God pleased, He could have made you one community — vie
with each in good.
From The Qur'an

Living a Metaphoric Life

Recently, while teaching a class on the kabbalah, one of the men participating in the session, listened intently to a woman sharing an experience of having opened herself to metaphoric possibilities in her life. Somewhat shyly, she described a very personal story of her shift from *Chronos* to *Kairos* through the appearance of a tiny but intent blue jay whose appearance she interpreted as a messenger. The bird's presence at that moment brought her a clarity she was seeking — the necessary synchronicity of an internal and external event, confirming something of significance for her. Whether anyone else would have felt that pairing as a connection is irrelevant — for her, there was a personal correlation with a broader reality. After the class, the man, contemplative and earnest said the reason he had signed up for the class was that he too wanted to learn to connect to this deep and mysterious realm described by the woman. It was so foreign to him.

How do we learn to trust, to look and listen? Perhaps examples are the best teachers, and such opportunities for affirmation are most easily relayed by the stories of our lives. In fact, the completion of this book came as a result of my being open to life's metaphors. Over fifteen years ago, I started working on this project and beyond writing an outline and a few sample chapters, realized that I was not ready to do this. I had an idea of what I wanted to write, knew how to start but had no idea where to end. Many years of life's experiences intervened, and several years ago a strange series of coincidences led me back to my passionate endeavor that I had needed to put aside for some years.

Invited to talk to a group of women about the biblical matriarchs, I discovered a circle of friends I now consider to be my soul-sisters. They had been discussing Sarah and were interested in the thoughts of the local rabbi's wife. By the end of the morning, our hostess shared a dream she had the previous night — one of those repeating dreams she experienced many times in her life. The dream images she shared sounded so strangely familiar, reminding me of something I had once written years before and had almost forgotten. I searched and found the story that appears in this book entitled *In the Beginning* — the title itself a metaphor of rebirth!

I shared my story with my new friend and she too was amazed at the similarity of images. She then gave me a story about Adam and Eve that she had written years before. Again I was amazed at the parallels in our thinking that had inspired my *midrash, Eve-o-lution: the birth of humankind* included in the appendix.

Re-reading *In the Beginning* after all those years was the impetus I needed to turn back to the writing of my book. "Coincidence" that I was invited to this group? That my friend recounted her dream from the night before we met? I have no logical explanation as to why we both felt a strong recognition of one another and the similarities in our life journeys. Being open to the possibility that there is a significance to the unfolding of these events, served as a very personal invitation to get back to work and complete what I had started.

The Mystic Within beckons us to live richer, fuller lives. She is informed by the intuitions, beliefs, thoughts, and feelings that surround her as she formulates her way in the world and encourages her sister, the Humanitarian, to action. Together, their vision, rather than just a dream, is a call from the potential just beyond our grasp. Gently reawakening the dormant aspects of our older right-brain perceptions and beginning to value their input on the stage of our inner lives, the dream can become the new reality we create. Just as we trust our five traditional senses as interpreters of our reality, we can open to these additional perceptive skills we have been conditioned to distrust, or worse, close down. Our own interpretation of the physical world creates our reality — we see the world not as it is but rather as we are.

Judaism teaches deed is more important than creed. At the

same time, we are not "human doings," we are human beings and our actions should spring from the deep, timelessness of our spiritual nature. Cohesion between the two is essential for ethical living. Belief should motivate the actions that bring about the changes necessary for the healing of our world. A sound sense of self is the start. The words of Hillel remind us: "If I am not for myself, who will be for me; if I am only for myself what am I? And if not now, when?"

Appreciating the gifts that we have to share with the world, and feeling good about ourselves, we need to make sure that our care and attention are not directed only towards ourselves. Such behavior is selfish. We need to care for each other. As instructed by the prophetic injunctions, for example, the conscious individual needs to "care for the widow and orphan, to feed the hungry, clothe the naked, celebrate with bride and groom, and console the bereaved." And there is no better time to start than right now.

Judaism encourages the search for the sanctity of each moment. Recitation of blessings brings Divinity constantly to consciousness, encouraging each one to become the blessing. This can be achieved with the understanding that the world depends on our actions. More than just saying the words — we are instructed to perform *mitzvot*, sometimes understood to be good deeds. They are commandments by which we are instructed to live, the vows we commit to uphold as the basis of an ethical life. A good deed that has an optional quality — if I feel in a good mood, I may give something to the homeless woman I see on the street; if I am not feeling charitable, I won't. An ethical principle implies that there is no choice in the way we respond. We act righteously, with kindness and consideration for others at all times.

When the human family behaves in this fashion, we hear the call of the Sacred Feminine encouraging us to usher in the messianic age of peace, a reality in which we will once again live in harmony with the Earth and with each other. Do we believe that such a vision is possible? The answer must be a resounding "yes" from the Jewish perspective, which, eternally optimistic, accepts the imperative to choose life and celebrate it. We need to seek the opportunities to live this reality.

Reality/realities?

The optical illusion is a great example of finding a teaching in the most unlikely of places. As children we are fascinated with a drawing that appears to be a goblet. As we look at the shape, it suddenly changes before our eyes. It is not a goblet — it is two faces looking at one another. How could we have ever thought otherwise? And then, magically, the goblet appears once more. As we watch, we find ourselves able to shift back and forth between the goblet and the faces. Which then is "real"? Background or foreground? The answer, as with any paradox, is both. We just cannot see both at the same time. Quantum physicists tell us that the sub-atomic world functions in the same way. We can observe two seemingly opposing realities that appear to co-exist — we just cannot perceive both at the same time.

Using the optical illusion as a metaphor for our lives, are we able to tune in to the broader reality, shifting our perceptions to a less well-known but equally valid experience? Or are we so fixed in our left-brained approach to life that we believe there is only one way — the literal and exclusively logical approach to living? Perhaps the visual experience of moving from one reality to another most readily comes to mind in the optical illusion. We can experience this shift in other ways too, for example, the moment we venture from our man-made, cacophonous, concrete culture and into the blissful silence of the natural world.

I remember one amazing day at Yellowstone last winter when a blizzard from the previous day had left the Earth blanketed with deep pristine, sparkling snow. My husband and I made our way from the Lodge through the drifts to Old Faithful and were able to watch its eruption, miraculously alone with the geyser in all its magnificence — except for a herd of bison, white-faced, from foraging beneath the snow. We stood in awe of Nature at her most majestic, and the silence of the experience, interrupted only by the occasional snort of a bison. A coyote noiselessly padded past us, seemingly oblivious of both the bison and ourselves. The words of Rabbi Abraham Joshua Heschel came to mind — if we are not awed by Nature's grandeur and cannot sense the sublime, however vaguely, when outdoors, we are not fully human.

Whenever we take time to step out of our human-made reality and into Nature, we confront silence — and it moves us, deeply. Civilization is noisy — from the machines on which we rely to keep our world of form going, to the chatter in which we engage endlessly, not only when together but even when alone. We become aware of that internal voice chirping away, commenting, criticizing, reminding, evaluating and judging. A profound experience in Nature makes us aware of the difference between silence and sound, as well as time and timelessness — two of the less obvious dualities between which we walk in search for balance, and of which, most of us remain largely unaware.

What if we as left and right-brained individuals, blessed with the many ways of perceiving multiple realities in our lives, are cursed with the ongoing patriarchal belief that we can only function in an "either/or" paradigm rather than a "both/and" possibility?

The right brain is the hemisphere of shimmering surprises which color our lives. How often, as we slip from *Chronos* to *Kairos* and back, do we experience a synchronicity and shrug it off, forgetting the adage mentioned previously, that coincidence is Divinity's way of remaining anonymous? How many other messages from Divinity do we miss? How many hunches go ignored? How many times do we experience inexplicable moments of ESP in a day? How many times do we know who is calling before we pick up the phone and dismiss it as "just one of those things" instead of appreciating the gift we possess to experience a broader reality? How many of us pay attention to our dreams? Would we consciously choose to leave an email from Divinity unopened?

That greater, broader, deeper reality is the ocean in which we blindly swim. Every now and then we bump into something that makes us open our eyes for a second and we marvel at this other reality, until Commander Left Brain calls us back to egoic attention, reminding us to get on with the work at hand and leave behind the foolishness.

Years ago in my first marriage, I experienced a momentary lifting of the veil that exists between the two realities. In Johannesburg, the city of my birth, I was in the car with my ex-husband (to whom I was still married at the time) driving past a beautiful park called "The Wilds." In retrospect, the name of this location adds a splash of humor to the experience! I turned to look at my husband and for a fraction of a second, it seemed I entered a crevice in time. I heard an inner voice ask who was the stranger driving the car, and more importantly, why was I with him? In a flash, the experience ended. It was as if a veil, momentarily lifted, dropped back into place. Everything appeared normal again, but I felt shaken and perplexed, wondering what had just occurred. I knew something extraordinary and mysterious had happened and had no logical explanation for it. I remember the experience vividly leaving no doubt I had momentarily crossed some threshold. In retrospect, and considering the marriage ended at a later point, I understand that the experience could have been an early awareness that I was not where I was supposed to be, and could not accept, at that point in my consciousness. I was not with my *beshert* (intended) although at that time I do not believe I could have confronted that possibility.

Do we find portals to enter the spiritual realm or do they find us? They exist everywhere and all the time. The first prerequisite to finding them is our own curiosity as we follow in Eve's footsteps. The second is the belief in the possibility that they exist. With such an attitude we learn to question everything we have been taught to believe is true.

Our world-view is set up in polarities. Kabbalah, the spiritual and inner teachings of the Jewish tradition, encourages seeking a place of balance between the two extremes and refraining from placing fixed value judgments on either, which we habitually do. What have we done to the polarity of light and darkness? We feel comfortable in the light and distrust, even fear, the dark. Rabbi Lawrence Kushner says in his book *River of Light*:

Without the dark womb of sleep, there could be no sensation of light, emergence of consciousness, or place to which to return. In the darkness there is no arrangement of past and future, no self-reflection, no ego, no neurosis. . . all genuine creating must originate in the darkness. All transformation must commence during the night. . . you cannot predict what will happen in darkness.

My personal ritual for honoring the mystery of darkness takes the form of planting seeds. Each year, I take the seeds of the *etrog* (the citron, a citrus fruit that Jews use during the *Sukkot* festival) and plant them in a flowerpot on my kitchen windowsill with the intention of sharing the tiny seedlings with everyone at the *Tu B'Shvat* (New Year of the Trees) celebration in January or February. It seems a natural bridge between one festival and another in the annual cycle of Nature festivals, allowing me time for reflection when the natural energies ebb as the winter approaches.

As I water the seeds, I recall the work of author Masaru Emoto. His photographs, taken through powerful microscopes, show frozen water crystals that seem to change shape and appearance according to human thought forms in their proximity. These photos remind me of the experiments reported in South African author, Lyall Watson's book *SuperNature*, popular in the 1970s. He reported the differences in growth rate of sprouting beans if love and attention were devoted to them as they germinated.

I send positive energy to the seeds as they start their journey to life. I keep watching the dark and fecund earth in which they rest, away from the light and my curious eyes. I wonder about the mystery of life. Will any of those seeds sprout and if so, how does the miracle occur? It seems I have to wait forever and suddenly, mysteriously, the first tiny shoot appears. Within a few days, more fragile green leaves break through to the surface. Out of the darkness comes light and life. This tiny miracle repeats annually on my kitchen windowsill.

Just as the seeds sprout in the darkness in a miraculous manner, the opening to spirituality does not come with the light of intellectual surety; it comes from the darkness of not-knowing, a recognition we feel rather than think. The first day of the biblical creation story reminds us that The Divine created light from darkness, order from chaos. Then on the fourth day, the sun and moon were created as lights in the heaven by which we mark the hours and seasons. What then is the first amazing burst of light with which cosmologists agree that the Universe began? Universal Consciousness? Out of the chaos of the multiple possibilities that are inherent in darkness, consciousness — before the heavens and the earth were formed and certainly before there were people? Teilhard de Chardin, twentieth century Jesuit paleontologist and philosopher, suggested that life on this planet is an evolution of consciousness that begins from the seemingly inanimate. Cosmologists such as Swimme concur, reminding us that we are all composed of stardust. Accepting this possibility, we can resonate with the predictions of the many psychics and futurists who believe we stand at the edge of a major shift in our evolution that is drawing us towards a level of consciousness unlike anything the human family has yet experienced. Perhaps the discovery of a quantum reality of deep connection heralds the way.

In a search for an interconnected conscious awareness, westerners pack the ashrams and retreats of India (including Jews in sufficient numbers for the Dalai Lama to comment on what a soulful religion Judaism must be, based on the number of Jewish Buddhists he meets on his travels!) There is a thirst for spiritual knowledge that remains unquenched by intellectual gifts and materiality. So we turn to spirituality, a most confusing word, referring to a world of multiple possibilities. It is the fourth dimension of life, the potential for connection and relationship with something integral, broader, deeper, and infinitely vaster than ourselves. It gives meaning and significance to human existence as the force that raises consciousness to a level of awe, and offers the possibility of a relationship with the Source of Being. Spirituality is the prism through which we can learn to see the ordinary as extraordinary; it encourages us to live in a state of gratitude. Such living is not limited by the outer rituals of different faiths but is the common wellspring from which all emerge and through which we can learn to see and celebrate our diversity in the mythic and archetypal themes we share.

The Tree of Life: Key to Jewish Spirituality

One of the portals to spirituality is the teaching of kabbalah. Its main tenet, in common with other spiritual traditions, is to find a place of balance in which to live a meaningful and successful life. To understand what is meant by a place of balance the kabbalistic Tree of Life — the *Eitz Chaim* — is a model for us to examine and consider. As shown in the diagram, it appears to be a design of geometric shapes, composed of three columns, ten focal points and the pathways that connect them to each other. The same teachings can be sketched in the form a *menorah* — a seven-branched candelabra on a three-fold base; it can also be drawn as an overlay of the chakras of the human body. Here, the Tree is used as a diagram of the way we function as human beings. It can be adapted for multiple other uses.

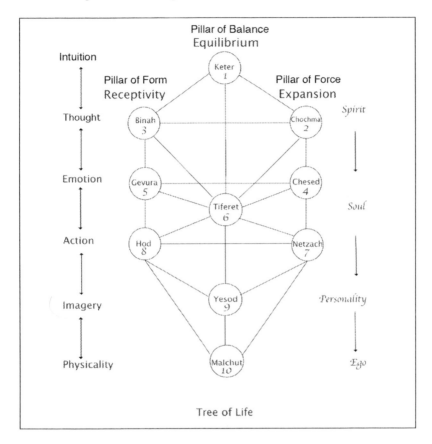

Tree of Life

The two outer columns, Receptivity and Expansion, represent the extremes or polarities in our lives, between which life energy continuously runs, with a central column or path of balance between them. The focal points are called *sefirot*. The diagram is a flat, two-dimensional representation of an organic structure that demonstrates the separation, movement, and containment of energy that keeps the whole structure alive. This symbolic energy flow is described in constant movement from one column to the other, from one *sefira* to another.

On the left side of the diagram, we can see different levels of accessing and processing information from physicality to intuition. This placement is not meant to be hierarchical in any way. Each level represent different aspects of ourselves. To the right of the diagram, the column from spirit to ego represent increasingly denser fields of vibration that reflect the layers that clothe our individuality within our physical bodies, allowing spiritual beings to function in a material world.

There are others ways of describing the energies of Life. In Eastern thought, the *yin* and *yang* energy forces circle and swirl in and out of one another in the eternal dance of life. *Sefirot*, pathways and columns — all are of equal importance in the understanding of the movement and containment of life's energy that Eastern thought refers to as *"chi."*

Kabbalists have used the Tree to explain the creation and nature of the universe and our part in it, focusing on the destiny of humankind and the attributes of Divinity as a teaching to help us find meaning in our lives. Kabbalistic concepts are built around the Tree of Life and the Four Worlds and deal with our relationship and aspiration towards Divinity, as well as the journey of the soul in human form. The imagery they use is borrowed from the sacred texts of Judaism. We need to constantly remind ourselves that these images are merely symbols for the Unknowable, and like the Tree of Life, are fingers pointing towards the moon — not the moon itself.

Our world, they teach, evolved out of Divinity's wish to experience Itself, and with that wish, came physicality. From the limitless Oneness, a beam of light penetrates the darkness of all that was, is and shall be, to unfold the first of the ten stages of creation called *sefirot* on the Tree of Life. Symbolically, these jewel-like blossoms on the branches of the Tree represent fragile vessels, containers of the sparkling light of possibility.

The Divine energy flows to fill the first *sefira*, *Keter* or Crown, to overflowing. The gentle, sparkling waterfall of Light or consciousness rhythmically, softly, fills each subsequent vessel to shimmering capacity and then overflows into the next waiting vessel or *sefira* on the Tree. The light moves downwards as it sways from one side of the Tree to the other, from the Pillar of Force or Expansion to the Pillar of Form or Receptivity. Each vessel colors the light that it holds and influences the container beside and below it — an ephemeral, spiritual rainbow coalition!

Energy is the Force, the *sefirot*, the Form. Between these two Pillars is the third called the Pillar of Balance — the only one in direct connection from above to below and back — the bridge between heaven and earth. Movement and containment of the Divine flow maintains its own intrinsic balance. This flowing and containing of Divine light passes through ten stages of evolution until the Tree of Life is in place. For the kabbalist, this process is repeated four times, once in each of the four worlds just as Divinity desires, conceptualizes, organizes, and creates.

To understand better we can think about how the human creative process of the visual artist repeats and models this pattern. The artist starts with the inspiration to paint. Then comes the thought about the "what" of the painting. Organization will involve the choice of materials and subject matter, influenced by experience and feelings. Finally the process of the work begins — the adding to and subtracting from the original strokes in balance with the wisdom to know when to stop. A new work of art is born.

For the mystic, the creation story in Genesis is pure poetry — consequently, metaphoric rather than literal. This story talks of the creative impulse of Divinity as described in human terms. The first "day" involves the birth of the light of consciousness from unconsciousness. This brings the potential of seeing an order in what appears to be chaos. Force is set in opposition to Form. Light appears in contrast to the dark, setting the stage for the dualities of human life.

The term "days" is cosmic — referring to vast periods of time as understood by us. The second "day" brings the dividing of the firmament between the waters above and the waters below, a metaphoric description of the next stage — a separation of the world-to-be from its source by means of an etheric shield that can tone down the vibration to allow the physical to manifest. Days three through six describe the ordering of the heavens and the earth, the setting of the stage for the play of Life in physicality. And finally, Divinity, pleased with the creation, acknowledging that is good, blesses it.

The mystical metaphors used here come from the teachings of the sixteenth century mystic, Isaac Luria, known as "The Ari." He described the separation of humanity from Divinity in terms of the shattering of these fragile vessels which, unable to hold the light, broke, causing the scattering of the Divine sparks. These shattered sparks of the Divine dwell within every living being as the source of our connection with Divinity. As ego development overshadows spiritual awareness, the sparks become encased, as if covered by shells that need to be cracked open to release the inner light. Contained within, the sparks still commune with us as the small voice within that reminds us to find the truth about ourselves, our journey, our purpose, and our home.

As bearers of the scattered sparks, our mission is to find our way back to the unity of the central flame of life and repair the shattered vessels, recreating the wholeness that was. This process, mentioned before, is *tikkun olam*. To do this, we need to experience physicality, learning through our personal life's happenstance to voluntarily make soul choices in alignment with the Divine Will. In this way, Divinity experiences the delights of the physical through us — cells in the organs of consciousness in the Divine Body. Divinity needs us, just as we need Divinity. As it is not possible for each soul to know all that life has to offer in a single round of the miraculous cycle, the journey we call Life is perhaps best understood as a spiraling series of journeys or adventures that we undertake time and again until wholeness is attained.

Created as we are, in the image of the Divine, we understand ourselves as co-creators of the physical world. The term "co-creator" presents us with the miraculous opportunity of healing the world. The Grand Plan for each individual spark is to return to its source, knowingly choosing to do so, having experienced the dualities that are imperative for choosing. Without experience and choice, we remain in the innocence of our Garden existence, nascent consciousness still dormant within us. Eve is the spark that ignites the journey and is humanity's quintessential hero.

At one time these teachings were kept secret. As mentioned before, one had to be male, at least forty years old, and well-grounded in Torah to comprehend the meanings of the teachings. The patriarchal proscription discouraging women from the study of religious and spiritual matters is both anachronistic and exclusionary. Was there an innate male fear of women's honed intuitive sense that could easily lead them to a deep understanding of the concepts that gleamed beneath linguistic covers? Hearkening to the Sacred Feminine offers a new and inclusive interpretation of this ancient body of wisdom.

Is being forty years old a reference to one of the magical numbers in the practice of *Gematriah*, a form of mysticism? Numbers have significance and seemingly occur as markers in the texts. Forty may be such a marker. In the biblical text, Noah spent forty days in the ark. The children of Israel wandered forty years in the wilderness. This number may make reference to a kabbalistic teaching. The Tree of life consists of ten *sefirot*. The Four Worlds — Emanation, Creation, Formation and Action here represented by Intention, Thought, Emotion and Action — each replicate the Tree from the world above. Ten *sefirot*, four trees — the number forty! Does this imply that once we have experienced and balanced the dualities of the forty *sefirot*, we have reached a point of spiritual maturation?

Experience can bring the grounding necessary to understand

the inner teaching of the texts. In theory, having incorporated the knowledge of the physical world, we will not be thrown off balance by the enormity, complexity, mystery, and paradoxical nature of the miraculous working of the Universe.

We can speculate on the reason the hidden, inner teachings were supposed to be kept secret. Was it for the protection of the spiritually immature? Jewish legend has it that four scholars entered the Garden, the place of expanded awareness, to which the kabbalistic teaching beckons. As a result of the unfathomable visit, one died, another lost his faith, the third became demented and the only the fourth one survived. Without the necessary grounding, hidden wisdom can threaten the foundations of an apparent and accepted reality.

Was the attempt to keep the teachings secret merely political and typical of the hierarchical nature of an earlier time? Like the fruit on the Tree of the Knowledge of Good and Evil, was it "forbidden" as an impetus to whet our curiosity? Would this possibility be revealed by eating the fruit on the Tree of Life? As with all other fields of study, the participation of women and men together can only add to our appreciation of the mysterious depths that wait us.

Ten Portals to Symbolic Living

An adaptation of this Tree of Life can serve as a woman's pathway to living a symbolic life. In bringing such awareness to the ways in which we live our lives and the decisions we make, we are able to re-imagine the Sacred Feminine and reincorporate Her energy into our own.

Life is a journey of becoming. In this context, the *sefirot* are described as entrances to a richer, more meaningful life for which we strive. Based on the understanding of Divinity as a verb — in action, in being and in becoming, instead of using nouns to name the *sefirot*, I have taken the liberty of substituting verbs. This change will hopefully capture something of the unfolding nature of the essence of each *sefira*, in keeping with the evolving nature of Divinity and ourselves.

Traditionally the Hebrew names of the *sefirot* are translated as Crown, Wisdom, Understanding, Compassion, Judgment, Beauty, Glory, Victory, Foundation, and Kingdom. They represent attributes of Divinity we can see mirrored in ourselves. As contemporary students of this mystical pathway, we need to translate the Hebrew words in a more accessible way. Wisdom, Understanding, Judgment and Beauty may open to us relatively easily but what is meant by Crown, Glory, Victory, Foundation, and Kingdom?

Looking at the diagram, follow the creative energy from its source. "Crown" is Intention and Intuition, the place of all beginning. According to the mystical teaching, in becoming manifest, energy moves through the Tree in a zig-zag fashion from right to left and then downwards, through each of the layers and *sefirot*.

Beneath Wisdom and Understanding, Compassion, Judgment and Beauty, all terms that easily reveal a context, what do we make of "Glory" and "Victory" placed at the level of physical action? In this context, I suggest the terms "Futurist" and "Herstorian" as I visualize a playful, spontaneous and innovative energy moves from a place of novelty, towards a more traditional sense of convention that holds impulsivity in check.

This seems fitting when we recognize a sense joy and humor as part of the Divine plan. Using "futurists" and "herstorians" at this polarity, we visualize an egalitarian future in which we need to add "herstory" into the record of the past because we are well aware that it was not recorded. Such revision may be troubling to those who view such innovations as problematic; I feel it is in keeping with the multi-layered possibilities of this ever-unfolding paradigm. Foundation and Kingdom are more often associated respectively with the imaginal and physical realms, as described in the work of many contemporary mystics.

Here, as an egalitarian pathway to wholeness the *sefirot* are named as portals to becoming. Spiritual sojourners strive for the ability to become inspired/inspiring, intuitively wise, understanding, compassionate, strong, beautiful, futurists, herstorians, dreamers, and sacred activists.

1. Becoming Inspired/Inspiring

Inspire. Aspire. It all starts with the breath. Just as we are told that humanity comes into being by the breath of Divinity, we know without breath there is no life. Many meditation techniques focus on breathing as a way to center and open the connection between ourselves and the hidden realms. Earlier, it was suggested that with conscious attention on the very mysterious and life-giving process of inhaling and exhaling, we utter the unspoken name of Divinity.

Taking some time out of each day to be still allows us to rest in the silent darkness in which new things can be born. Inspiration starts with being present in the now, freeing ourselves of existing, absorbing memories of the past or anticipations of the future. The Hebrew word *hineini* means more than "I am here" — it implies being fully present, attention alert. Removing ourselves from the clutches of *Chronos*, we stand at the portal, leaving the horizontal marking of time, and plunging into the vertical depths of *Kairos*. It is from this place of inherent stillness we sense all things are possible. It is in such states that intention can manifest; with intention we can set the tone for the coming day or for the rest of our lives, one day at a time. We can try to start each day by asking the question: How do we want this day to unfold? By visualizing an expectation for the day, our intention can assist us to meet the daily challenges with equanimity.

In the stillness we can take stock of ourselves and analyze what we are doing to impact our world for positive change. How much energy and time — those most precious commodities — do we waste on worrying about things that have not happened, and may never happen. The future is yet to unfold in ways that are unpredictable; the past is the place of memories of things that were. Each breath we take can bring awareness to the present, where our attention needs to be, in order for us to focus on how we are living our lives.

An old aphorism reminds us: "where attention goes, energy flows." As we look for inspiration and consider becoming a source of inspiration for others, we need to become conscious of where our attention is directed. We need to gently call it back to the now. Inspired ourselves, we can be inspirational to others. Who is the role-model of the qualities we admire? Most often, it is not those whose names are famous or whose faces we recognize from television.

We can all think of people we know in whose company we feel good — energized, engaged and happy. What is it about them that make us feel this way? Is it their inner stillness we can feel, an unruffled ease in dealing with life and situations, the ability to smile even in the midst of challenges that they do not allow to become all consuming? Is it the compassion they feel and manifest as they find ways of making a difference in the chaos of life? Perhaps it is the wisdom evident in the decisions they make, exhibiting an awareness of history and an ability to project into the future. Is it the way in which they create a sense of harmony around them or the fortitude with which they face challenges in heroic ways, being able to place one foot in front of the other when the difficulties confronting them seem overwhelming? Is it their sense of appreciation — for life, beauty, Nature, and relationship that enriches us in their presence? Some people inspire us by the persistence they exhibit in following a goal of making the lives of others better.

As we consider the qualities we aspire to manifest, we can think about such people and what draws us to them. Perhaps we sense the Sacred Feminine a little more substantially through them. Many of these qualities we learn from the interconnection of attributes on the Tree of Life. Like most things, they start in silence, in the absence of the sounds and sights that constantly impinge upon us. Our lives are so filled with noise and images — auditory as well as visual, especially in this "e-age" in which we are continually bombarded by stimuli. In addition to going within to find the stillness, we need to find ways in which to create quiet in our outer lives too. How do we develop these qualities?

We can start by making use of the off buttons on our televisions, computers, and radios. We need to filter what we are taking in daily, sometimes unconsciously (both in sound and sight) of the chaos around us — chaos that we can see, hear, touch, taste, and feel. We can choose to read selectively, if at all, from the barrage of negative news stories assaulting us daily, as well as making it a practice to read some inspirational poetry or prose each day. We can find something of beauty at least once a day and to stop to really look at it — a sunset, a favorite photograph, the face of a loved one. We can choose to smell the fresh cut grass. We can savor the taste of the food we eat instead of eating unconsciously as many of us do. Too often our attention is focused on those with whom we share our meals — or the television or book on which we concentrate, unaware of the flavors of the food that nourish us. We can start to feel the difference in textures around us. Gently touch a loved one. How does their hand feel in ours? We can burrow our hands deep into the soil or let water run through our fingers. We can feel the velvety texture on the back on a fallen leaf. When we are fully present in our lives we exude a calm that is palpable.

Do we become what we desire? An understanding of the universal power of attraction makes us aware that the time spent on thinking about the things we do not want, as well as the things we do, paradoxically draws both to ourselves. We set up our own self-fulfilling prophecies — how often do we expect a parking place exactly where we want one, and find it waiting for us?

How many of us focus on what we support, rather than what we are against? Mother Theresa is reputed to have said she would not attend anyone's anti-war rally but would be part of any rally for peace. It is helpful to know research shows an athlete's body responds in the same way whether she is actually engaged in her sport or just visualizing being active. As we think, so we create; as we are, so we interpret the world to be.

Thinking of those we consider role models, we can imagine ourselves feeling and acting as they would and following through on such actions. In the presence of young children we need to be aware that they are carefully watching us as they formulate their codes of behavior. If there is a difference in what we say and what we do, they will imitate what we do.

Edgar Cayce taught that "mind is the builder, and the physical is the result." In wishing to become inspiring, we need to constantly fill our minds and imaginations with those thoughts and images that propel us to act for the highest good at all times. In this way we are able to bring godliness to Earth and help ground Divinity in physicality. In Shakti Gawain's phrase, "for the highest good for all concerned" could be equated with do no harm.

Judaism teaches that we are to become the blessing. Constantly reciting blessings, we remain in a state of consciousness, appreciative of the gifts we possess that we often take for granted. Reciting blessings is a way of expressing words of thanks to Divinity. On waking up each day, we say, "Thank you, living and Eternal One, for returning my soul to me in Your compassion." This is the first of the hundred blessing we can say daily.

We give thanks for the working of our bodies, for the wonders of the world, for our relationship with loved ones, and for the opportunity to act as Divinity's agents for good in the physical world. Learning about the traditional recitation of a multiplicity of blessings that the traditional Jew is encouraged to do, can help anyone reformulate the communication between ourselves and Divinity in ways that are meaningful. By constantly expressing appreciation, we move into a place of gratitude for everything we experience — including those things we find unpleasant or painful — often things we cannot understand. We learn to expect that they too will come into our lives and learn to look for the gifts of inestimable worth that such challenges bring.

Conscious breathing, stillness, filtering out what we take in, finding words that inspire and move us because of the beauty of the images they create, choosing to bring beauty into our lives — all help put us in touch with inspirational sources that in turn will assist us to become inspirational to others.

2. Becoming Intuitively Wise

Stop. See. Hear. If we start with the assumption that there is an invisible world of connection underlying everything we perceive through the five senses, we open to the possibility of finding that point at which the two realities, the horizontal visible and vertical invisible, intersect.

The alchemists believed in the "unus mundus" — the inter-connected world in *Kairos* concealed within the material world. For some of us, the connection between the two is most real through our dream images. For others, it is an awareness of the numerous synchronicities that — like hummingbirds — magically and momentarily flit into our lives and disappear, adding sparkle to the bland monotony of routine and leaving clues to the connectedness of all things. The more we start to notice and appreciate these gifts, the more they seem to appear.

We can enjoy the humor that synchronicities bring. My teacher, Alice O. Howell encourages all her students to remember that Divinity has a sense of humor. A few years ago, while preparing a talk I was to give on the subject of intuition, I remem-bered an audiotape I had purchased featuring Dr. Judith Orloff. I thought it would be helpful to listen to her wise words once again to create the mood I wanted for the presentation. Since I was to be in the car for a couple of hours, I thought I would have the perfect opportunity to listen. I could not find the audiotape with her name on it anywhere. I was puzzled and frustrated because I knew that I had it. Aggravated and running late, I grabbed another tape as a second choice that I had purchased from the radio show, *New Dimensions*. I hadn't heard this tape for some time. As it started, I heard Dr. Orloff being introduced and I laughed out loud. Intuition works! I had forgotten she was a panelist on the tape I owned. I had been searching for a tape with her name on it. Talk about intuiting a talk about intuition! How can we not enjoy the humor?

Developing our intuitive wisdom encourages us to break out of old ways of seeing and look for the signs that come our way. Books fall open on certain pages — or right off the shelf in front of us while we are looking for something else we thought we needed; there are signs from Nature that indigenous peoples readily understand. Everything we need to know we can learn by closely observing Nature — for example, if we take the same route on a daily walk and revisit the same plants and trees, we start to notice subtle changes that tell us about the process of life, death, and rebirth all around us.

I noticed a calla lily on my walk each day. I marveled at the unfolding of the first flower on this particular plant that I was just learning to appreciate — I had previously thought these flowers stiff and unyielding. I was beginning to see a swirling elegance in the bloom. As the days passed, I was saddened to notice the first signs of discoloration that preceded its withering. Before it died, another flower started opening, repeating the cycle of life in the same plant. This is a great metaphor for our lives as we consider our own mortality. We enter life through the portal of birth and exit through the portal of death. One generation makes way in time and space for the generation that follows. From *The New Union Prayer Book For The Days Of Awe*, comes this moving passage:

> If some messenger were to come to us with the offer that death should be overthrown, but with the inseparable condition that birth should also cease; if the existing generation were given the chance to live forever, but on the clear understanding that never again would there be a child, or a youth, or a first love, never again new persons with new hopes, new ideas, new achievements; ourselves for always and never any others — could the answer be in doubt?

Everything in and about the physical world is temporary. We experience it for the span of a single lifetime. If we expect permanence from the flow that is continual, we sow the seeds of our own unhappiness. Being temporary, everything in materiality changes. Awareness of the metaphoric level of existence serves as a reminder of the deeper and eternal level of continuity in which our souls dwell. Paying attention to the metaphoric possibilities of our lives opens us to experiencing life more fully. Opportunities for such openings occur in the most unexpected ways.

Years ago, shortly after emigrating to America I first started reading about pre-patriarchal culture. I was intrigued to learn that the priestesses at Delphi kept snakes whose venom, it was believed, was used to induce trance states necessary for the giving of the oracles. Coming from South Africa where most snakes are extremely poisonous, I was terrified of all of them. On this particular day in the late 1980s, I was teaching a group of potters the art of oriental brush painting. It was a full-day workshop at our home. At the lunch break, the participants went onto the deck adjoining the kitchen. Someone came in to tell me there was a snake on the grass. My immediate reaction was the conditioned fear I would have expected. Then I thought about what I had been reading. I went out onto the deck, and there below me, resplendent on the grass was a magnificent emerald green and black snake.

As ludicrous as this may sound, I felt she waited for me. I saw her, she saw me see her, and in a flash she disappeared. I had never seen her before and never saw her again in all the years we lived in that house. A synchronicity between something in my inner world and my outer experience came together for me in a most powerful way. I recognized its significance for me at that moment in time. It was a gut-level knowing that had nothing to do with intellect. Was this just a "coincidence" — or a sign acknowledging the intuitive truth-filled sense of what I was starting to understand?

Becoming intuitively wise means starting to interpret our lives metaphorically and symbolically. A friend shared the experience of visiting a healer. My friend has a hearing loss she had learned to live with, which was not the purpose of her visit. She had made the appointment regarding another health issue. The healer felt the need to work on her client's hearing anyway, which she did. During the session, my friend remembered a time in her past when she was dealing with difficult circumstances and responded with the words "I don't want to hear any of this." At the end of the session, not only was the memory intact, but a later appointment with an audiologist revealed that she had regained a twenty decibel increase in her hearing acuity that maintained itself for some time.

A good place to start opening to the wisdom of the Sacred Feminine that comes to us all, seemingly uninvited but welcomed, is to start being open to the possibility of such connections. Keeping a notebook in which to jot down the synchronicities and signs of which we become aware is a great way of saying *hineini* — I am here and paying attention. Wisdom is not merely the accumulation of knowledge. Wisdom comes from experience in the outer world as well as from connections to ancient sources from within. Wisdom can temper knowledge and guide our application of what we know.

Medical science has developed the ability to do amazing things and often the question becomes not one of "can we" but rather "should we?" Examples come readily from the issues that medical ethicists confront. Mastectomy is a radical procedure that can save lives. Should a teenager carrying the genetic blueprint giving her a fifty percent chance of developing breast cancer be allowed to undergo a double mastectomy to prevent the possible disease? A fifty percent chance is not a guarantee that the disease will occur, and ten years from now, there may be other effective and less radical ways of treating it. At the same time, we can understand the desire of a young woman not to have to undergo what other family members have endured or worry that the disease may appear.

Raising children gives us many opportunities to exercise wisdom instead of knowledge. In answering the questions they ask, we learn to discern the amount and quality of the response we should give. A humorous example comes to mind of the five year old who asked her mother where she came from. Thinking this was the cue for the beginning of her sex education, the mom started to explain. Her daughter, looking puzzled interrupted her saying that her friend came from Michigan, and what she wanted to know was where she came from.

Indigenous people gain knowledge of the natural world through experience and observation of their place in the natural order, rather than through academic learning; such knowledge is handed down through the generations. Such sharpening of perceptive skills may play an important role in honing intuitive senses.

3. Becoming understanding

Opening to our spiritual dimension is about learning to live in a state of non-judgment. Accepting there are the polarities we can list such as good and evil, right and wrong, we can learn to stop adding values to the duality. How often do we hear that out of adversity comes the most unexpected reward? From illness or injury, a new career or avocation; from the dissolution of a long-lasting relationship, the start of one much more suited to the maturity we have reached.

Buddhism teaches us that our tendency to attach ourselves to materiality or even our expectations, brings us suffering in the form of discontent. If we expect nothing from anyone, we will never be disappointed and each good thing will be a surprise. The behavior of others towards us can be a source of pain. If we can detach from any expectation or outcome in any relationship, that does not involve violence, we distance ourselves from possible hurt.

Strong in our own belief about what is acceptable, we can move away from hurtful situations when necessary. Feeling good about ourselves, we project that sense of well-being — and start to discern similar patterns in those around us. Those who engage in destructive behavior towards others — in words or in deeds — are not feeling a sense of self-comfort and their hurtful and destructive behaviors reflect this disturbance. A sense of self that is unthreatened, allows us to hear from both sides of any issue with compassion and then to understand something of both sides.

We can think of the stereotypical case of sociopaths, who through personal experience as children, or some imbalance within the physical mechanism, learn to control their own environment in ways that are destructive to the self and to others. We can learn to see the genesis of such behavior, and without condoning the actions, understand its roots.

Understanding draws in its wake the ability to forgive when the need for forgiveness is apparent. Judaism teaches that although all human beings are born good, we constantly err in judgment and need to understand what is harmful to ourselves and others. We all need to redress the wrongs we create.

Forgiveness is a major theme of *Yom Kippur* (The Day of Atonement) and the High Holy Days. Jewish tradition explains that in order to be forgiven by God we first need to make amends with those we may have wronged. Bearing a grudge, resentment or animosity weighs us down. Ultimately, we comes to understand forgiveness as the process of release from these heavy burdens from the past that we carry into the present. When so weighed down, one allows anger, disappointment, betrayal and our diminishment by others to capture and hold our attention and become the filter through which life is viewed.

Psychotherapists easily recognize that anything causing us to act out by pushing our existing buttons of fear, anger, denial, judgment and projection are signs that the unconscious Shadow, as described by Jung, is at work. He described two aspects to this Shadow world, one personal and individual and the other, collective — belonging to the human family. We struggle to understand the Shadow in either aspect because it is unconscious, unknown.

The Shadow can be linked to the creative, dark and murky depths in which our symbols and dream images are birthed. If we struggle to understand the language of this realm, it ultimately becomes decipherable. It is like traveling in foreign countries whose alphabet forms are different from our own. We know how frustrating and alienating this feels to one who cannot interpret the shapes.

The symbolic images are intrinsically without value, being neither negative nor positive. It is within the unconscious dark that the creation of the new and novel occurs. Sadly, so much of our culture teaches us to fear the dark; we feel less afraid when we can see, and then understand, what we confront. For this reason, we have trouble trying to describe or understand the contents of this inner, unknown realm.

Instead, imagine the collective unconscious as a yet unlit subterranean passageway to all that our human family ever was, is, and shall be — the composite of every experience, thought, feeling and imagining we have had, are having, and will experience. For Jung, this is the collective unconscious; Eastern spiritual teachers talk of the *akashic* record. This symbolic ocean is available to all. To approach it, we each venture through that corridor of our own personal unconscious. The experience does not have to be frightening.

In the course of our soul's journey through life, we box up the unpleasant personal challenges and experiences we cannot face or own — the humiliation, shame, guilt, and fear we experience as human beings on this spiritual odyssey. These are the seeds of our personal unease. We store these boxed memories in the basement into which the tunnel opens. The boxes scare us and gain power because of their unconscious contents that we cannot bring into the light. The memories, although our own, become estranged from us, unloved and unwanted aspects of our own experience. However, we recognize them immediately in others and react negatively to them in the outer world. Once we are able to meet these alienated memories at a more matured time in our lives and bring them back to the light of awareness, they are no longer Shadow. If we accept the idea of the unconscious as a passage-way into the "all that ever was, is and shall be" we can venture into this unknown world. The fabulous treasures that await us are unimaginable. If we can understand (even by whistling in the dark) that nothing we have stored in our basement boxes can retain the power they once had if we can open them to the light, perhaps we may be willing, with support, to venture downstairs, with a light in hand, to sweep away the darkness.

There is absolutely no doubt that humanity's cruelty towards other members of the human family considered "other" leaves us in great fear. Earlier, we looked at the enormity of the Nazi Holocaust. How much time is needed to incorporate the immense grief in its wake? It is a question that seems impossible to answer. Jewish prayer-books suggests "to brood over our sorrow is to embitter our grief. Our task is to serve and bless the living." Where is the line drawn between coming to terms with what happened in Europe just sixty years ago and the ability to move forward? Post holocaust, world Jewry is forever changed. How does one deal with the holocausts that tragically continue to plague the human family all over the world?

It was Hillel who said: "Whatever is hateful to you, do not do to any person. That is the whole Torah, the rest is commentary." The phrasing of this statement in the negative encourages us to behave in this way for no reason other than it is right — non-harmful to self, others, or the planet.

Starting to look at and understand our own foibles and eccentricities, we come to terms with accepting ourselves; from a place of self-worth and self-esteem, we can approach one another without judgments and learn to appreciate the difference and uniqueness which makes the spectrum of the whole human family so fascinating.

4. Becoming Compassionate

Compassion is the practice of unconditional love. We can learn to become more compassionate by refraining from standing in judgment of others. The adage to love our neighbor "as" we love ourselves may be easier to do when we translate the Hebrew to read we should love our neighbor "because" our neighbor is just like we are. Our "either/or" paradigm has reveled in separation and stratification. Everything is valued as "better than/worse than." By opening to our innate sense of compassion, we can learn to celebrate our diversity and so sanctify life.

In the years before I had my own children, I was in practice as a speech therapist. I remember my first experience with a child who had been physically abused. As I was preparing to meet with his mother for the first time, I was filled with righteous indignation at her treatment of her son. After that interview, I was humbled when I realized she was acting out in the only way she knew how, as she had been treated by her parents. Understanding does not mean we condone such action but it does temper our judgment of the perpetrator.

In addition to the collective provinces of pain and suffering, we all endure personal experiences of wounding. As we evolve into the maturity of our later years we realize, at different points in our own spiritual growth that we each need differing spans of time to deal with our individual trauma. Medical intuitive Carolyn Myss has been a wonderful spokesperson on "woundology." On the individual level she shows that some people find it almost impossible to let go of the things that have wounded them and these painful experiences become an essential part of who they are.

Having experienced my own share of pain that has shaped me, I know how difficult it is to let go. I believe we reach a point of release when we accept the past as past and look toward a new day, changed by our experiences, but ready to choose life. How long this takes us to achieve is ultimately an individual decision, once we become aware of the trap of being stuck in the past and unable to move. It is not possible for any outsider to try and change or speed up the process. We all come to learn there is only one person whose behavior we can change — our own.

Understanding and compassion are close allies, as are wisdom and understanding. All address life from the sense of inspiration connecting us to the greater reality and mystery of which we are a part. Understanding life as part of this enigma is wonderful. As finite human beings, we cannot see the whole picture. Learning to dwell peacefully in the unknown and unknowable offers the opportunity to release the struggle in which we engage as we try to understand. Thomas Moore's superb best-seller *Care of The Soul* "just happened" to come to me at a time I really needed to read his words.

This book helped me to understand and appreciate the

mystery of life and the fact that sometimes there are no answers to life's challenges — in this case, why adult human beings can hurt one another as we do. The book struck a chord with me and I was able to eventually let go of my personal anguish.

We can learn to practice compassion for those who are suffering. Neither an attitude that pities nor patronizes — compassion instills within a deep empathy for those in pain. We learn to be discerning rather than judgmental. Understanding that the grand mystery of life may elude comprehension at times, can be the first step in assisting us with the evolving acceptance of life that can grant us peace.

Of all the qualities associated with The Sacred Feminine, perhaps it is compassion that most people name when describing this Presence. Once awakened, we are cannot help feeling the plight of the other and unbidden, try to be present for them and if appropriate, to find ways to lighten their burdens. The more compassionate we become as a human family, the closer we are to a Messianic era.

5. Becoming Strong

Women need to own their intrinsic strength and allow its expression in spite of the societal fears of women's power. The adage "women who don't make waves don't make history" is something to consider. There are times we need to be confrontational to protect ourselves or others depending on us; there are other times in which a quiet certitude, gentle in nature, allows us to remain firm in keeping with what is believed.

Many women in my generation and before were taught to believe in their own innate weakness. Many younger women flaunt their strength by emulating power in the masculine form they observe around them. Somewhere between these two polarities is the feminine path to power that we can learn to walk with dignity. This has more to do with empowering oneself and others than the idea of "power over" others.

A quiet refusal to do something we don't wish to do, in many instances, is more effective than allowing ourselves to become emotionally charged. When the emotions run high, it is almost impossible to hear the intuitive voice. If a situation calls for anger, we can wait until the emotion settles before trying to sense our inner wisdom. Intuition is found most clearly in unemotional, creative silence.

Contemporary women need strength to maintain the many roles they play. Often the needs most neglected are our own. In providing for all around us, we feel that taking some time for ourselves is selfish. Judaism teaches ego has a place in all of our lives. We need to be able to care for ourselves in addition to those who depend on us. When boarding an aircraft, we are told in case of emergency to first take the oxygen mask for ourselves before helping another. Good advice for life too.

Standing up for what we believe to be right, being able to say no when appropriate, remaining committed to ideals even when not shared by those in our immediate circle are not traits that come naturally to many of us. They are however options we can learn to exercise. Being part of a women's group is often very helpful in this regard. Women share stories, and by listening, learn.

Strength is what is required when any one of us face those challenging times that come to us all. Being able to find a way through and to see, that no matter what the circumstance, "this too shall pass" is very difficult, and calls on all the fortitude we can muster — often just to get through one day at a time. During the moments of crisis or challenge it is hard to see just by taking the journey itself, we win the prize. In the heart of each of the deepest personal pains, resides a seed that can blossom into a gift of unimagined value.

Sometimes, acting in strength means staying still, saying nothing and holding the space for a loved one to live their own life and learn the valuable lessons that come from dealing with pain. How challenging it is to watch those we love struggle and suffer. In compassionate strength we learn when our assistance is helpful and when it is best to stand back and love others through their difficulties.

Once we understand that life provides us with the opportunities the soul requires, the most painful and unwelcome ones usually bring the greatest gifts for our own soul growth and sustenance. It is so difficult to see this when in the midst of the struggle. With a little distance and perspective, as we return to our normal lives, changed by the experience and able to move on, we begin to see what we have learned and how we have grown. The Sacred Feminine gives us the courage to be bold.

6. Becoming beautiful

Beauty is easier to recognize than to define. For the mathematician, it may be the elegance of a simple equation; for the musician the contrast of a single note against the silence that precedes or follows it, to the artist the play of light that suddenly manifests and changes the nature of a well-known object. However we attempt to define beauty, our souls are touched by it in some inexplicable way. Beauty is far more than a perceptual experience. It is the way our perception makes us feel as we connect sensation and emotion and a wordless sense of gratitude. Most of us are deeply moved by the beauty inherent in the expression of love — a grandmother's smile as she watches a grandchild, lovers re-united at an airport, the look of achievement on the face of a child who manages to finally accomplish a goal that has eluded her. We can see physical beauty in each other, from the deeply lined face of a wise elder, to the naive expectation on the face of a toddler. The amazing differences of face and form and the variety of races and colors that make up the human family exemplifies the beauty found in diversity and treasured by The Sacred Feminine.

Real and eternal beauty has very little to do with our outer selves — our aging bodies, height, weight, coloring, or sense of style. So much of our attention goes to keeping our surface appearance all we think it should be. We want to be as attractive as possible. There is the amusing anecdote about the woman who was asked if she would rather be attractive or intelligent. Without a moment's hesitation she replied she would rather be attractive as men see better than they think. Surface and substance. Where does real beauty lie?

The physical body is the container of the inner self. Surface characteristics may be important but not as significant as the substantive inner qualities that compound rather than confound attraction. In our memories of much-missed loved ones who are no longer alive, what is it that we remember most fondly? Probably not the exact color or style of their hair, the shape of their nose or the shirt size they wore; more likely, we recall the intangible aspects of their personalities, their idiosyncratic sense of humor, their unique soul essence we sensed through their expressions and the quality of their love and attention they gave us, and how they made us feel when we were with them.

Soul essence gently invites us to become all that we were destined to be — the unique individuals we are. We are asked to develop and enhance the talents we were given and to learn to soften the edges of the ego-centered needs and emotions that keep us from connecting with others as intimately as we might wish. We can learn to modify and eliminate the protective shields we develop that ultimately separate us and cause distress to ourselves and to others. There is an adaptation of an old Jewish adage that when we die we will not be asked why we were not Beethoven, Shakespeare or Renoir; the question we will be asked is why we were not ourselves? We each have a specific role to play in the drama of human life.

Life can be challenging and stressful, and we try to learn to keep balanced and centered in order to function as well as we can. There are many ways we can learn to find an inner stillness, and the practice of meditation is a popular one. Spending time doing the things that totally grab our full attention — reading, or following the avocations on which we focus completely, allow us a mini-vacation from our daily lives that refresh and center us from the stresses that pull at us and cause us to feel fractured.

From a place of inner peace, we can readily share a smile with others — even when under pressure. It is a contagious activity and tangibly alters our environment. The resulting connection we feel with each other opens us for warm communication. We all know people in whose presence we love to be — we just feel better when they are around. We respond to their inner beauty that enhances our own.

The inner beauty or harmony we strive for is enhanced by the way we learn to accept ourselves and take chances to follow the goals, aspirations, and vocations that bring us joy. Many of us assume happiness and joy are the same sensation. Joy is a deeper, richer, more substantive acknowledgement of being in tune with life. It knows no opposite. Once we feel it, we recognize joy as our birthright — that center point from which we move and to which we long to return in the journey of life. This deep emotional state of well-being puts us in touch with the sense of wonder we experienced as children, and on the occasions we are able, to cross the threshold into the timelessness and limitlessness of *Kairos*. It is perhaps the idyllic state in which to experience Divinity.

Many of us find we experience joy most readily out in Nature or when we bring Nature indoors. We are deeply moved by the grandeur we experience as well as the intricacy of the details at which we marvel — from the fractal patterning of Nature, to the iridescence of the butterfly's wing, and the gigantic trunk of the sequoia whose age and presence defy understanding. I feel a sense of joy by having fresh flowers in our home at all times – a single flower in a small vase or a bunch of wild flowers that makes our house into a home.

Surrounding ourselves with objects that please us — living entities such as plants or animals, or objects and sounds formed by human creativity, all bring us pleasure because of their intrinsic beauty or because of the memories they hold. They are so important in bringing harmony into our lives as we try to create a place of beauty in which we enjoy spending time. Playing the music we love also helps create an environment of beauty that soothes the soul. Treating ourselves with regular time to meditate is another source of pleasure.

We can learn new skills and find where our own creativity lies. The great philosopher, Martin Buber, reminded us that every human being has the urge to be creative. This applies not only to the arts but also to the way we live our lives and solve our problems. Involving ourselves in some creative endeavor also puts us in touch with the inner metaphoric life from which we draw sustenance and enter the stillness.

Learning to responsibly use and respond to all of our multi-layered emotions may perhaps be the *raison d'etre* of human experience, as many spiritual teachings suggest. We are not certain what emotional states other life forms experience — those of us who have dogs cannot help but be aware of their response to our emotions and the depth of the unconditional love with which they shower us. As human beings we can bring awareness and choice to the state of our feelings and emotions and in so doing, we gain some level of efficiency and mastery over the way we react to our environment, so filled with opportunities for pleasure or pain.

7. Becoming futurists

Quantum physicists teaches that space and time as we understand them, are constructs — merely tools we use to place ourselves in the stream of our lives. Past and future may be illusionary as the present moment is all we ever have. We can learn to consciously visualize the future we want by seeing it in the present moment and use the laws of manifestation to bring such goals into our reality. Creative visualization really works. I remain joyfully convinced my serendipitous meeting with my husband thirty years ago resulted from this practice.

Months after my divorce was final in 1977, and familiar with the book *Creative Visualization* by Shakti Gawain I carefully thought about the qualities I would like to see in my next life partner — I knew I did not want to remain single. My written list showed he would be a spiritual man, intelligent, emotionally stable, with a ready and kind sense of humor. He would be good to my children and to me. He would be willing to go to Temple with me. Three months later Rabbi Norman Mendel came into my life, two weeks later we were engaged, and thirty years later to the day as I do my final revisions of this text, the rest, as they say, is history. We need to be very specific in creating such a list however — Divinity has a sense of humor! When I added to my list that I wanted some-one who would go to Temple with me, I did not mean every week!

I had known about manifestation before I found the words to describe this process. I recall as a child I had heard by looking intently at a cloud one could intend it to dissolve. Not believing this for a moment, and intrigued with the challenge, I remember lying down on the soft white sandy beaches of the South African Cape Peninsula and staring upwards. I would select a small cloud and would concentrate on it. It dissolved. Would that specific cloud seemingly have dissolved anyway? Without anyone watching, who would have known? I still have no idea of whether or not it was an illusion, or how to explain what I was seeing. I became interested to know more.

As a teenager I started to drive, I would find parking spaces where I needed them. I got to see my name on the "Student of Year" board at my High School, after deciding, for some obscure reason that is what I wanted to see. Many students that year got better grades than I did, but I received the award I had visualized. In retrospect, I have no idea why it was so important to me — other than perhaps seeing it as an affirmation of the process.

Reading Gawain's book was one of those experiences of immediately recognizing her words and what they were saying — that feeling of "oh yes, I know that! So that is what they call it." We can all learn to create aspects of our lives by the laws of attraction — according to the mystics, this is what the human experience on Earth is all about. We are told we do this unconsciously anyway, so why not bring awareness to the process? *Creative Visualization* is a wonderful guide to developing these skills.

As futurists, we can envisage the world, the nation, our families, and ourselves as we would wish them to be. Plato created a Utopian society in *The Republic*. Many visionary novels attempt to do the same in a more contemporary setting. *He, She and It* by Marge Piercy and *The Kin Of Ata Are Waiting For You* by Dorothy Bryant are examples. They imaginatively recreate the world and set the possibility of different and interesting challenges for the characters. We can ask ourselves what the ideal society would be and start acting as if we are living in it.

Reform Judaism teaches that humanity is not waiting for the arrival of a Messiah to solve the world's problems; we are working towards a Messianic Age in which we all act and respond in messianic fashion. Poet and author, Danny Siegel says it perfectly:

If you always assume
the one sitting next to you
is the Messiah
waiting for some simple human kindness —
You will soon come to weigh your words
and watch your hands.
And if that person so chooses

not to reveal him or herself
in your time —
It will not matter.

If we treat everyone with whom we come into contact with the gentleness and kindness we would the Messiah, we will help to bring on the Messianic age.

8. Becoming "Herstorians"

To understand the story of human evolution on this planet, we need to add "herstory" to our reported history. I have shared some of the ways we can come to find the whispered voices of our foremothers and amplify their sounds to learn from their experiences.

There is an abundance of books by women scholars, as well as painting, sculpture, music and lyrics created by women artists. Women are now in place in almost every profession and career, and we can find wonderful role models among us. We can think about the women who have influenced us, those we know personally, and those we know from their work or creative endeavors. We can think about why they appear heroic and try to incorporate some of their values into our lives.

Judy Chicago is a contemporary artist and poet whose work speaks to the soul of the evolving feminist. Hillary Clinton maintains her composure on the stage of public life as she uses her intelligence and will to create a better world. Debbie Friedman lifts our hearts with her inspirational music as she adapts the lyrics from Jewish religious tradition to be sung with her original music. Author Irshad Manji shares her feminist journey as a Muslim. Oprah Winfrey may personally have touched more lives for good than anyone else on this planet, past or present. Maya Angelou, author, poet, and singer, teaches about the dignity of womankind. Mother Theresa lived a life of selfless devotion to humanity.

On a personal level, among my friends are many women who have accomplished and continue to accomplish so much, creating new and amazing ways of being. I think of the many artists, musicians, writers and poets I am privileged to know. Many are using the advantage of living in an American open society to fulfill themselves in different walks of life. Within my own circle, a friend was recently ordained as a Roman Catholic woman priest, another white American woman was trained as a *sangoma* by South Africa shamans; I enjoy the company of a medical intuitive who is Wiccan, a Muslim physician who was raised in a Hindu family, Jewish women who practice Buddhism, religiously non-affiliated women who are drawn to Hindu theology and meditation, and several Christian friends who have left the tradition in which they were raised and are now inter-faith leaders of those who no longer feel comfortable within the confines of normative and institutional religion.

We can all bring to mind unsung heroines of our worlds, forging new paths and lighting the way for others who will follow. Theirs are the successes we celebrate as we become role models for others. In sharing our stories, we remember who we are, as barriers dissolve and we recognize the Universal Woman within — reflections of the Sacred Feminine.

A distinctly Jewish setting for celebrating "herstory" is to gather as a women's circle. *Rosh Chodesh,* an ancient festival with biblical roots has been reclaimed as a time for women to meet on a monthly basis. Unlike other women's groups who meet for full moon meditation, Jewish women meet at the New Moon, symbolic of a fresh beginning at the start of the new month on the Hebrew lunar calendar.

At such a gathering, women share stories and expand the awareness of our contemporary experience as women. In appre-ciation the of multicultural diversity surrounding us, when facil-itating such get-togethers, I have chosen to follow a theme that offers a lens of feminine wisdom and intuition as a way to examine the month just past and set goals for the month about to begin. We have taken books by different women writers, not all of whom are Jewish, and we used their material for an annual cycle of *Rosh Chodesh* gatherings. We see how their teachings apply to our lives. For example, one year we used Carol Pearson's *Awakening The Heroes Within; Twelve Archetypes to Help Us Find Ourselves and Transform Our World*; next we used Rabbi Shoni Labowitz' book *Miraculous Living: a Guided Journey in Kabbalah through the Ten Gates of The Tree of Life*; the following year we read and interpreted *The Thirteen Original Clan Mothers: Your Sacred Path to Discovering the Gifts, Talents and Abilities of the Feminine* by Jamie Sams.

Our monthly gatherings begin as we light a candle to mark our entrance into *Kairos*, that sacred time-space in which we will share our stories. After a short silent meditation, we use the following prayer that I wrote many years ago specifically for this purpose:

Creative Spirit of the Universe, *Ruach Ha-olam*, Source of light and love, guide and bless us on our journey as we gather together to meet, to share and learn. Help us truly to see, to hear and feel, and so experience the reality of our lives. Help us to become discerning rather than judgmental, acknowledging the perfection of life even when we do not understand or intuit the strands that make up the perfection of the weaving. Assist us to be with each other in peace and always to respond to one another with love and respect — particularly when the reality out of which we function is different from that of others. May we be guided to become full participants in the joy of living that by our thoughts, our words and our actions, we help to make this planet a little brighter and lighter for our having been present. May we always be conscious of our roles as instruments of Your peace. Amen.

We go around the circle and each one introduces herself and names her mother and grandmother, and as many of those of preceding generations she can; some mention the names of daughters and grand-daughters as well. We each end the introduction with the word *"hineini"* meaning "I am present" signaling to ourselves and others we are ready to listen to and learn from one another. We do a second round, in which we share something of our lives over the past month. Because the groups normally include women from their early twenties to those in their late eighties, we share experiences that cover the full range of feminine experience.

We then look at the coming Jewish month from many different perspectives — traditional, mythic, and mystical. The discussion for the gathering will often come from the book we are reading for that year. We use the thoughts and the ideas they birth as a way to examine our responses as Jewish women.

Finally, we enjoy a silent meditation and a prayer for healing and close the circle by extinguishing the candle and reciting a closing prayer:

Shechinah, Source of life, light and love, *Eloheinu,* fountain of fortitude and faith, we bless and thank you as we unite your energies within ourselves. We intend to be clear vessels for your light. Energize and enable us to play our part in *tikkun olam.* May we reinvest enchantment in our lives, bring peace into our communities, healing to the human family, and respect for all life as we learn to celebrate the diversity around us. Amen.

Such groups provide bonding settings for women, supporting and encouraging each one who is part of the circle. The group offers a monthly gathering, spiritual in nature that grounds everyone in community. At times, we have prepared creative *midrashim* (storytelling that fills in the gaps in biblical stories.)

Once tried, we know we will never again read the original tales in the same way. The characters seem to come to life, relating their lives and their stories in ways we can feel.

To try this, choose the characters from selected stories that fascinate the group. Ask the questions that draw us into the tale. In the appendix, I have included two of my own *midrashim* — one about Eve, the other about Abraham, as well as a story, *Timeless Celebration* written in the same vein — this one not based on a specific text, but rather in response to questions about the connection between women's rights and rites.

9. Becoming Dreamers

Just as we can connect with the intuitive realm by following our hunches, celebrating our telepathic moments, recognizing and enjoying the coincidences that come our way, nightly we encounter a dream life that sleep offers up to us. This symbolic realm opens to us as a personal, bottomless treasure-chest of surprises, creative solutions, and humorous metaphors that connects us with all others, past, present, and future. From ancient times, as the Bible attests, messages from the dream world have shaped the lives of the dreamers who pay attention to this creative inner world.

There are many books we can read and courses we can take that will assist us in interpreting the images of our dreams. For those of us who, in the morning, remember nothing of this alternate reality, there are ways in which we can train ourselves to keep the memories alive by noting them in a dream journal. I enjoy the books of dream analyst Jeremy Taylor who poetically describes the many baffling images we struggle to describe as "not yet speech ripe."

Most dream experts encourage us to keep dream journals in which we develop the habit of transcribing whatever we can recall, even if all we can remember are dream fragments. It is a useful practice to write the dreams on one side of the book and keep notes on the opposite page about events of the day before, the associations of which we are aware that may connect to the dream images. Most important are the emotions we felt during and after the dream.

Keeping such a journal is fascinating, not only from the insights we gain from single dreams. Themes emerge over time from our dream lives, illuminating the personal metaphors we use in our waking lives. The emotions we recall are good clues to the meaning of each dream, specific to the dreamer, coming as it does from each individual personal unconscious.

In striving towards adding the dimension of symbolism to enrich our days, our dreams (daydreams, night dreams, repeating dreams, and precognitive dreams) are truly gifts we receive. We need to honor them as connecting bridges to Divinity and the metaphorical life.

10. Becoming Sacred Activists

Judaism teaches its adherents to take a stand, to make a difference, to try to make the world better because we are in it. As we mature, we understand that no one can focus on all the tragedies of the world that beset us, or those individual and group tragedies that can break the human heart and spirit. Their details bombard our senses as our world becomes smaller through the use of the technology. We cannot deal with it all, but neither are we free to do nothing.

Choosing one issue that speaks to us, about which we feel passionate and motivated to find ways to ameliorate the problem, places us on a path of moderation, encouraging a sense of balance. We face issues pertaining to the environment, war, nuclear proliferation, abuse, discrimination, hunger, illiteracy, and the sex trade that enslaves the weak and the poor, mostly children. We see a corporate consumerist greed that sacrifices indigenous cultures and "expendable" people on the altars of avarice benefiting the few at the expense of the many. These are just a few of the issues that confront us at the start of a new millennium and a new age, all important and worthwhile causes. Jean Shinoda Bolen's book *Gather the Women and Save the World* includes so many shining examples of women helping women, one person at a time, as we find ways to change the status quo. Micro-loan organizations like www.kiva.org, www.partnershipway.org and www.womenforwomen.org are a few of the worthwhile organizations that provide us with the opportunity to help.

The empowering of women is basic to recreating an egalitarian society. The arena of women's roles and rights as a global issue is where I choose to make a difference. These are issues about which I feel passionately. Even though we may have been blessed in this lifetime not to have personally experienced discrimination or harm because we are women, we feel the injustice of this form of discrimination — be it in Afghanistan or right here at home.

I support women's causes financially and as a spokesperson where the opportunity arises. For a number of years I was the Public Affairs Associate for Planned Parenthood because I believe that the education and services they provide to maintain repro-ductive health are the keystones to a better society, nation, and world. As a woman learns about herself, her body, and her rights, she will understand the sacred importance of parenting. If she decides to become a mother, she will recognize the time at which she feels that she will be able to become the best mother she can be for her child, not only at the moment of its birth, but in all the years that are to follow. A child that is planned and wanted is welcomed into this world. Surely it is the birthright of every human being.

Whatever causes one wishes to support gives us the oppor-tunity to stand up and be counted. This is what *tikkun olam* asks humanity to do. Jewish wisdom reminds us: "It is not ours to complete the task but neither are we free to desist from it." As a human being, one feels compelled to make a difference, to try in some way to improve our world.

For me, everything revolves back to our understanding of Divinity and our expectations from that relationship. We can find ways to develop and fulfill the potential we have. Incorporating the teachings of the Tree of Life helps set a roadmap for the journey.

Knowing God as process, ever-evolving, continually present and constantly changing implies we can hold on to whatever image of Divinity feels supportive and loving and brings us a sense of peace. As we grow, our images will change while The Presence remains constant. In this way the watchword of Judaism: "*Sh'ma Yisrael, YHVH* is our God, *YHVH* is One" is profound. Far more than a statement of belief in a monotheistic God, the implication is that what we worship is the Oneness of all creation. With this understanding of the nature of Divinity we can appreciate and respect the images of others as valid and important parts of The Whole, differing images or labels that no longer challenge or threaten us in any way.

As women and men acknowledge and appreciate one another in love, The Wholly One is joined with The Beloved, The *Shechinah* — as below so above, and as above, so below.

By learning to acknowledge our understanding of Divinity and appreciating the images of others as being of equal merit, we can look at each other, eye to eye, and in that gaze find The Divine Presence alive, loving, and whole, and we can say Namaste, Salaam, Peace, *Mitaku Oyasin, (Native American affirmation "we are related")* Shalom.

Conclusion

My personal journey has taken a different path from anything I could have visualized. From my childhood in South Africa I was aware of what discrimination did to both the oppressors and the oppressed. There was no way of knowing that my focus would shift from racist to sexist discrimination. As my interests in Judaism and feminism appeared to be on a collision course, I was able to find a way of appreciating both, and finding value and worth in bringing the two together in an approach I call egalitarianism.

In the early stages of questioning my faith, I felt discomfort. Over my left shoulder, it seemed, I could feel the imagined disapproval of the long line of purported rabbis in my paternal family line. Together with the generations of men who created the patriarchal garment that clothed Divinity in the Jewish tradition, I could see wagging forefingers and could hear the whispered word "*shande*" (scandalous). I could also feel, over my right shoulder, the gentle caresses of the generations of women whose lives provided the foundation for my physical experience as a twenty-first century woman. Kindly smiles on ancient, wrinkled faces encouraged me to go on. This feeling has always been enhanced and strengthened by the support and encouragement of my amazing husband and partner.

My feminist and egalitarian conclusions have not interfered with who I am as a Jew, anymore than the treasures of my Jewish faith diminish my belief in the value of labeling myself as an egalitarian feminist. As we enter this millennium and "new age" I believe we will create a fresh paradigm of synthesis to replace the divisiveness of the past two-thousand years. I hope we will make connections between the disparate parts of ourselves as we bring our religious and spiritual selves into a sacred relationship within. This is the meaning of *shalom* — the real peace that comes when we are not feeling fractured and when we attain a sense of wholeness.

I am grateful that my Reform Jewish practice is open-ended enough to encourage me to question everything and return with new insights and ways of finding my identity within my religious tradition. Judaism has given me a love of learning and the belief that it is important to follow my dreams. It constantly reminds me I need to take part in repairing the world in my own unique way. I acknowledge the identical spark of Divinity existing within each and every human being and at the same time, savor our uniqueness as individuals. There never was anyone exactly like you or me and there never will be. Identical and unique, at one and the same time. Through our individual insights and participation we add our own contribution to the record of human experience, and in this way connect Divinity and Earth as was intended.

I thank all my religious, feminist, and spiritual teachers, women and men whose thoughts have made me reassess my role in my community. Their shared insights are the jewels woven into the warp and woof of this tapestry. They have brought light and beauty to my life. It seems the time has arrived for the Sacred Feminine to re-awaken and rise. As we look at the present condition of our world, we can see where living without this principle has taken us.

If, as the opening verses of Genesis remind us, the creation of the Earth was good and is for good (in both senses of the word — meaning beneficence as well as eternal), we have within us the potential to live good and creative lives. As maturing partners of The Creative Source of Life, we can find ways of living in kinship with each other and the planet. We need to see the patterns and connections that abound and find ways to make the necessary changes to live in harmony with the Earth and its network as well as the human family. To do this, we need to awaken from our unconscious, automaton-like state. We cannot afford to remain asleep in the depths our own unconsciousness.

Holding that image of an evolving Divinity, *ehyeh asher ehyeh* (I will be that I will be) is for me, a profound reminder we are created in the image of this constantly present and continually changing God, Divinity as process rather than product. We have the innate ability to grow, to stretch, to change, and to become more than we are at present. From the *New Union Prayer Book* comes the following quote adapted from words by Emerson:

> "The gods we worship write their names on our faces, be sure
> of that. And we will worship something — have no doubt of
> that either. We may think that our tribute is paid in secret in
> the dark recesses of the heart — but it will out. That which
> dominates our imagination and our thoughts will determine
> our life and character. Therefore it behooves us to be careful
> what we are worshipping, for what we are worshipping we
> are becoming."

Owning our own potential assists us to recognize one another as
spiritual members of one family. Harmonious living is possible. It
calls to us to examine our own behavior — our feelings about
ourselves, our relationships with each other and the essential
need to come from a place of respect for our diversity.

From this vantage point, we are able to honor the natural
world that sustains us. Our mistaken hierarchical notions of
"having dominion over the Earth" needs to be replaced with the
understanding that we are here, on this human journey, as
caretakers of all that has been loaned to us. We are to live in
harmony with the natural world that sustains us. Opening to the
Sacred Feminine, we realize we are all part of a grand and
connected whole. The potential for building a glorious future for
the human family exists. Dancing in the footsteps of Eve, we need
to remain curious and brave enough to step forward and reach
for the fruit, this time, ready and responsible to taste the fruit
growing on the branches of the Tree of Life. With the courage to
take what the Tree offers, we awaken to the possibility of recreating Eden here on Earth — a place of being, in connection with
all beings as we learn to celebrate our diversity and sanctify life.

L'chaim – to life.

Appendix

Creative *Midrashim* and other stories

I have included 3 stories – two are *midrashim*.

A *midrash* is a story that flows from the gaps in the biblical text; the additional story is just an imaginary tale based on Jewish feminist history

1. Eve-olution: the birth of humankind

Eve stood beneath the branches of the Tree at the center of the Garden. They surrounded her, protectively like the wings of those who sang so sweetly from the tree. She loved being here, at home, in the Garden. The glowing fruit was in her hand, warm, soft and inviting. She knew that the juice would be sweet to taste. Although time did not yet exist, here she was able to gaze into what would become the past and future of Earth's history. Once again she thought about her alternatives. She had been given the choice before, and she knew she would be given it again. Not eating would ensure that innocence would remain in the Garden. Innocence, she knew, was incomplete, inexperienced, and inert.

She looked at the warm, living fruit in her hand. The rosy blush of the sacred fruit was as pleasing to her eyes as its feel was to her hand. Eating of this gift of creation would open for them the gates of the Garden. They could step out into a material beginning. She looked at her beloved Adam. As the separated beings they would agree to become, they would experience loneliness. They would not be able to merge, as they could now, in this Garden of Oneness. Sexual fulfillment would be the closest they would come to knowing the ecstasy of merging.

Separation would be necessary because the material world on Earth would operate under the law of duality. The challenge for their children would be to find a place of balance between the apparent opposites they would experience, to find the Oneness from which they came. This would be the first exodus of many for the human family, whose mission would be incomplete until Oneness was attained. Physicality would bring the wonder of physical experience and emotion, as well as loneliness and even forgetfulness: to be totally present in their material world, their energies and attention would have to focus on the physical realm. She and Adam, her soul-mate and help-meet, would be the agents of consciousness that would bring the God-force into yet another level of existence. Adam comfortably deferred to her intuitive sense in matters of discussions with Wholly-One, just as Eve, he knew, would willingly follow his plan once the course of action was decided. Balance and happiness, you see, really did reign in that Garden!

Eve knew how she would be vilified by humanity in its infancy. For a time, many of her sons would consider her the most evil of beings because of her decision to start this journey. She knew that her wondrous intuitive sense, with which she communed with Wholly-One would come to be detested and feared. Intuition would be symbolized by the awesome snake — icon of wisdom and knowledge — which, like Eve, would become feared and demonized. Wholly-One assured her that although this early stage would seem like an eternity when they were in physical garments of skin, it would really be momentary. Time and space, after all, would be but illusions they would devise in trying to understand and to remember. Each would claim their Divinity when ready. Ultimately they would bless her and gratefully acknowledge her as their mother, the spark that started physical experience.

For much of its beginning, humanity would take literally all the allegories their priests and storytellers would invent regarding their beginnings, until the time for maturity drew closer and understanding of symbol and myth would softly edge into their consciousness. It would take humanity time to understand that this journey was a choice she and Adam were given by Wholly-One, who wanted them to undertake it — but only when they were ready. It had to be a choice of free will, which was the natural law in the Garden, as duality would be on Earth.

Previously, she had hesitated. Compassion for generations of her future children stayed her hand. She could see the road ahead, the blindness, the misunderstandings, the hatred, the pain and tears caused by their ignorance. Out of those painful lessons would come understanding and rememberance. She would be blessed always by Wholly-One as she was now. She knew what Wholly-One wanted from her when she was ready and now, finally, she was.

In joy and thankfulness, she put the sweet fruit to her lips, and savored its fragrance and flavor. This was the key to the Gates. She reached out and took another fruit from the sacred branch and giving it to Adam, encouraged him to eat with her. They once again discussed the odyssey they were to undertake. He was not sure he was ready for separation and the loneliness, for himself, or for their children. He grieved for the time in the story in which his sons would forget the "wholiness" of his daughters. Eve understood and lovingly encouraged him, knowing that every-thing would turn out just the way it should. She knew it was time.

Hesitating, he came to a decision. If Eve was ready, he would follow her intuition. He ate of the fruit she had brought to him. It was delicious. Savoring the wonder of it, he walked to the tree and took a second fruit. Eve knew that his eating twice from the tree would make memory more difficult for him but she would be there, at his side, to help him remember. In sleep and story they would have the opportunity to cast off their human forms and revert to all they really were. She, Daughter of Wholly-One gave thanks, honored and joyful to be doing what had been desired, but never asked, of her. She lay down next to Adam and merged with him once more, for the last time, the two becoming one — inner and outer, active and receptive, male and female, intuitive and intellectual, thinking and feeling, wisdom and understanding, compassion and discernment — all at-one-ment in the garden.

"Tomorrow" the adventure would begin. Eventually, they would return to the Garden, mature, whole, and fulfilled, having completed the task lovingly offered them. The wholly-one slept peacefully beneath the Tree of The Wholly One.

2. Father Love: a *midrash*

Abraham awakened with a start. Women were usually the Dreamers. When a man found himself blessed with the gift, as Abraham had before, he would bring the vision to the priestess in order to understand the fullest possible meaning of the mysterious symbols. Women were known to have easy access into the Dreamtime, just as men best understood Daytime. Abraham had always been happy to follow this tradition, until that fateful dream so long ago when he broke with tradition and decided not to share this dream with Sarah — the most highly respected oracle and interpreter of dreams. That fateful night, so long ago, he had dreamed he was to circumcise himself and all the males of the community, including his son Ishmael. He knew that Sarah would disapprove as it was not the way of their people. Hagar, however, would be delighted to have her son circumcised in the Egyptian tradition. The dream made no sense, but at the time, leaving their homeland had made no sense either.

Without any discussion with Sarah, he assembled the men, and starting with himself, he performed the rite on adults and infant males alike. The men complied even if they thought it as strange as he did because they believed that he and Sarah were being led by Divinity and they trusted their leaders.

When Sarah discovered what had happened, she was distraught. He had doubly broken with tradition — first by not consulting her and even worse, from her perspective, by introducing this foreign custom to their people. He had known these matters were their mutual responsibility. When confronted, he told her he knew she would disapprove of the circumcision. She reminded him that there were many ways to interpret the gifts from the Dreamtime. The incident changed their relationship and an emotional rift between them was created at that moment, softening over the years, but never dissolving completely.

With the birth of Isaac, as predicted, life had changed dramatically for them both. The miracle had occurred in spite of their advanced years. They had named him Isaac, as Abraham had been instructed in the single Dreamtime gift that he had received after the circumcision ceremony. Naming his son was strange too, for the women usually named the children. However, everything about Isaac's birth was different. The tension between the parents certainly lessened with the joy and pride they felt in this special child.

Abraham's pride in his two sons was enormous. He was content until Sarah realized that the time had come for the two boys to be separated. In her understanding of the Divine Plan, she knew that both of Abraham's sons would father great nations. Destined to be separated, their descendants would learn, over time, to make peace with each other. Was this not the way the world of dualities operated on Earth? To find balance, humanity would have to learn to walk between two opposites. Each son would represent one polarity, allowing humanity the opportunity to use the gift of choice with consciousness and responsibility. Early on, their separation would lead to fear and distrust which would ultimately turn to love as they remembered their unity. Wholeness would be restored. Their coming together, far into the future, would serve as an example of how all people could overcome differences and celebrate similitude.

Abraham was distraught and spent much time in meditation and prayer. Eventually he heard the *Bat Kol* — the sacred feminine voice of intuition — that reassured him. It encouraged him to listen to Sarah as he had when Sarah had first brought Hagar to him. The *Bat Kol* reminded him that they needed to work together as a couple and that Sarah's intuition was finely honed. Sarah, the *Bat Kol* reminded him, was a vital part of the unfolding Divine Plan.

Heartbroken, Abraham gave Hagar and Ishmael the provisions they would need and watched them go, heading out toward the desert. Abraham had tried to concentrate on the promise that through Ishmael, a powerful nation would arise which meant that Ishmael and Hagar would survive in the wilderness, in ways he could not foresee.

Over the years, not a day went by that his heart was not saddened by the memory of Ishmael and Hagar. Each time he saw Isaac he was reminded of his first son, now lost to him. After allowing Ishmael and Hagar to go, the relationship with Sarah had improved somewhat. She knew how hard it had been for him and she tried to be loving and supportive but the relationship was not as connected as it had been before the circumcisions.

And now this. Another terrible dream, this time involving his second son. What did this God want from him? Surely Isaac was not to be taken as well? He went outdoors to watch the dawn breaking in the east. He knew he should discuss this most frightening of dreams with Sarah. How could he? This time it was her son. Had he misunderstood this dream too? Surely Sarah would think so. Before going to bed that night, he had looked at Isaac. How like Ishmael he was becoming, now that he was growing into manhood. Was Ishmael this age when he left? Abraham could not be sure. He fell asleep thinking about Ishmael. Perhaps this bizarre request to take Isaac to the mountaintop and sacrifice him to God was a confused memory of the loss he endured with Ishmael's disappearance. Tired, troubled, challenged, and confused, he decided once more against consulting with Sarah. He and Isaac would go up to Mount Moriah as he believed the dream instructed. He would not tell anyone, including Isaac, any of the details of what would transpire as he did not want to appear as unsure as he felt.

Before Sarah was awake, he and Isaac assembled the men for their fateful journey. After three days, Abraham and Isaac separated from the others and went the rest of the way to the summit alone. Together they prepared the altar as Abraham had told the men he would do. Isaac, happy to be alone with his father, assisted with the construction. When it was completed, they sat down, father and son, side by side, and waited.

For what was to be the last time, Abraham heard the voice. The *Bat Kol*, mysterious voice on high, called out to him, softly: "Abraham. . . Abraham."

"*Hineini* — here I am. I am present."

"Abraham, why did you bring Isaac here with you?"

"In my dream you asked me to. . ." He hesitated to finish this sentence.

"Abraham, the Eternal delights in humanity and cherishes life. Do you really think you would be asked to take the life of your own son? Separation from Ishmael was very difficult for you. Your deep wound caused by the loss remains unhealed. The Dreams sent to reassure you, you chose not to remember. All these years you have carried a burdening guilt about Ishmael. Yet is he is alive and well, residing with his family in Paran."

"You . . . asked me to bring Isaac up to the mountain top?"

"Yes, but not to sacrifice him. We needed you to pay attention. You must understand that you did not sacrifice Ishmael. Neither will you sacrifice Isaac. Ishmael and Isaac will live and their children will be numerous as the stars. We wanted you to understand something of the nature of Divinity that you obviously did not believe. Had you chosen to speak to Sarah, she could have reassured you. But you no longer hear the sanctity of her words because of the unnecessary guilt that you have been carrying."

"My heart has been heavy these last years because of Ishmael. I hear what Sarah has said about the parting from my son and his mother — a part of me is gone. The feeling persists in my waking hours and when I am ready to sleep."

"The Eternal wants you to be at peace, with both of your sons, and with yourself. You were promised that your sons would father nations, and they will. Be of good faith."

Abraham looked at his son, sleeping peacefully at his side,

oblivious of his father's ordeal. Isaac was safe, as Ishmael was safe. How foolish he had been to doubt The Eternal. What would Sarah think of his assumption that The Creator would expect him to sacrifice their son and not share this dream with her for fear of appearing foolish? He could not face her. After sacrificing the ram they discovered in a thicket, he decided that when they came down from the mountain, he would go to *Be'er Sheva*. He would send Isaac to *Keriat Arbah* to Sarah, his mother. In so doing, he made the decision to separate himself from his second son knowing now both boys would survive. He could not know that Ishmael and Isaac would come at his death and together to bury him in the Cave of *Machpelah* as a sign to future generations to come together when the old ways died out.

The men were delighted to see Abraham and his son return together. They knew that Abraham had not taken a sacrificial animal with him on the last part of the journey, and for some strange reason, wondered if Isaac was to be the sacrifice? What an absurd thought! Thankful to the Eternal that Abraham and Isaac were back, the men started back down the mountain.

3. Timeless Celebration

The woman they called Chava smiled as she watched the candle flames dancing. Her heart was filled with joy. The ritual that they had created to link them to their past, both Jewish and feminist, had been completed and they felt filled, unified as a group of special friends, connected to their past of thousands of generations, and most importantly, connected to their Creator.

She was one of them, but not quite, for they did not know that she still remembered her soul essence as Everywoman All-Time. She was delighted to have been part of this "newest" of their rituals, devised to bless Tamar as she moved into her Wise Woman Way — the name they had chosen for this celebration to mark the passage into menopause. The group's genuine enthusiasm and joy kindled the flame that had always burned deep inside of Chava, a flame sometimes strong, sometimes flickering, depending on the cultural winds that blew in the time and place in which she resided.

Her memory took her back, beyond this time and place, to the Beginning-That-Had-No-End, when her consciousness first flickered into life. How quiet and peaceful life had seemed then. The clan resided in the plains of what is now known as Turkey. She recalled the first Wise Woman celebration of which she had been a part.

Although the words were certainly different, the feelings were the same. Their time together was one of sharing and caring, of identification with each other and their Creator whom they called The Great One. The group lived in closeness with each other and with Nature. Flowers, dance and song were as much a part of their rituals and prayers as were the oil-lights and the wine. Women and men shared in all rituals together, fulfilling the ceremonial roles required of them as they blessed all births, couplings, and deaths, as well as the life-cycle events that came in-between. Having witnessed childbirth, they knew the creative power of life within the female body; it was obvious that The Great One, the Source Of All Life was addressed as Our Lady and Queen of Heaven. Everyone knew that She was not like any mortal female and that the feminine language used to address her included everyone. She was a power beyond the limits of gender and the human body, and yet at the same time, close enough to be comforting in times of trouble. She was gentle and caring as The Mother of All should be and at the same time as firm as any mortal loving mother needs to be to discipline her children.

Chava's mind wandered forward in time. The chill winds of change had blown across this planet that she loved so dearly. Changing cultural beliefs had altered reality for women. She found herself in Uruk in Mesopotamia. She recalled the Wise Woman Celebration for Rachel; now, however, only women were present. Their men's minds had been swayed to believe that such rituals were evil, as were the priestesses who still taught of the Great One as Our Mother, Our Queen. In their newly formed fraternity, now some thousand years old, the men knew the Great One as a Warrior King and Judge who ruled with justice and mercy. They knew this, for like their ancestors before them, they were reforming their concept of the Great One in their own image. Chava and her sisters knew that their men revered this new image and had developed their own associations that excluded all women. The men now segregated themselves for prayers and rituals to their Father God. With this separation came hierarchy, and an "either/or" understanding of reality that replaced the ancient way of thinking which had included many alternatives.

Several hundred years later, Chava recalled Sarah's Wise Woman ceremony. They were living in England and the cold darkness in which they found themselves was more than physical. Not only were there no men present, but the ceremony was now held in secret, for such rituals were forbidden, as was any contact between women and their worship of the Great One. In order to survive, they had gone underground and although outwardly they paid lip service to the concept of a male god, in the sanctuaries of their own souls, they knew, they felt, and they understood their truth.

At the time when Rebecca should have celebrated this age-old ritual, Chava recalled, the women in the *shtetl* (village) in Riga had not only forgotten the ritual, but in their waking hours, filled with such hard physical labor, they had even forgotten that there should have been one. Chava remembered her feelings of deep sadness at that time, but knew she should be patient for the mighty pendulum was swinging, and was now moving inexorably towards a return, and to balance.

Chava, Everywoman All-Time, smiled as she brought her consciousness back to the present. She sat on this beautiful California beach with her soul sisters, the soft white sands beneath them, the sounds of the ocean in front of them, and the light of the new moon at this *Rosh Chodesh* above them. She watched the gently flickering candle flame casting shadows on the faces of her dearly loved companions as they quietly hummed the closing melody. Yes, it was all happening again — the companionship, the ritual candles, the flowers, the singing. Their unity as a group drew them closer to each other and their Creator, as in time past. The same — and yet different. It augured well for the future. Her smile turned into happy laughter as she hugged her sisters when the celebration for Tamar came to an end and they started to pack up their ritual items and prepared to go home.

Study Guide and Discussion Topics

- Is Eve a heroine or villain? Western religion believes in her villainy because of the way the creation story is told. She disobeys God. In this book a different Eve is described; furthermore, it questions whether women are in the process of taking fruit from the Tree once again. How does the book suggest this is happening? Does the idea of "disobedience to the patriarchal image of God" cause you any discomfort?

- God is constantly present and continually changing. How does this idea fit into your personal image of the Divine? What labels and/or images best describe the way to name and understand Divinity?

- God-as-verb rather than God-as-noun — how does this change your understanding of Divinity? What does the idea of YHVH translated as the pronounceable name, He-She mean to you?

- "Created in God's image" means many different things. What do you believe?

- What influences of the patriarchy define your life and influence the possibilities of the choices you make? What do the terms "either/or" and "both/and" mean to you?

- As you think back over your life, what forms of "exodus" have you made? Did the transitions that seemed most challenging at the time lead to changes that you now consider positive or negative?

- What does the word "myth" mean to you? How does the idea of measuring time in different ways — as *Chronos* and *Kairos* — affect your understanding of reality?

- What do you understand by the words pagan, witch, hag, crone?

- Stories have three aspects — the teller, the tale and the listener. Do you consider the biblical text to be the word of

God? What affects do the human scribes, redactors and translators have that may influence the way words are heard or read? Is the text open to interpretation? Has reading *Dancing In The Footsteps of Eve* given you any new thoughts about biblical text?

- What do you believe about idolatry as the mistaking of "part" for "whole?"
- What do you understand by the term "Judeo-Christian." Is it an appropriate term to use?
- Is The Sacred Feminine alive in your life?
- What steps can we take to help create a more inclusive, global family living in harmony with the Earth?

Glossary

Adama(h)	Earth
Aish	Fire
Aggada(h)	Story; way of interpreting the Law in story form, imaginative, According to the spirit
Aggadic	Adj. from aggada
Akashic record	A Sanskrit term for the records of everything that was, is and shall be
Am ha-aretz	Unschooled individual; literally, person of the Earth
Aliyah	Going up – to the bimah during worship; emigrating to Israel
Aliyot	Plural of aliyah
Asherah	Canaanite name for the Goddess
Astarte	Canaanite name for the Goddess
Anath	Canaanite name for the Goddess
Assiyah	Fourth world in the kabbalistic framework translated as Action
Atzilut	First world in the kabbalistic framework translated as Emanation
Avatar	Enlightened presence, descended form higher realm, Hindu
Avodah	Work; worship
Ayin	No-thingness
Ayin Sof	Without end
Ayin Sof Or	Divine beam of light
Bat Kol	Heavenly voice
Bereishit	Opening word of Torah; in the beginning
Beshert	One's intended or fated partner
Beth Din	Religious Court

Beriah	Second world in the kabbalistic framework, translated as Creation
Bimah	Pulpit
Bodhisattva	Enlightened being, Buddhist
Brachot	Blessings
Chag	Festival
Chanukka(h)	Winter festival of lights
Cherubim	Intermediary between Divinity and humanity
Chronos	Archetypal image used to measure and mark man-made time
Chutzpah	Audacity
Drash	Story or tale of enlightenment
Eheyeh asher eheyeh	I Am That I Am; I Shall Be That I Shall Be
Eitz Chayim	Tree of Life
Elohim	Hebrew name for God; plural suffix
Etrog	Citron; fragrant citrus fruit used symbolically at *Sukkot*
Fahribbel	Yiddish for squabble
Feminist	Anyone, male or female, who honors "The Other"
Gematria(h)	Assigning numeric value to Hebrew letters to obtain an alternative reading
Golem	An inanimate form, made animate by human beings; from Jewish legend
Haggada(h)	The story of The Exodus, retold every year at Passover
Haggadot	Plural of haggada
Halacha(h)	Legalistic interpretation of the Law; literal; according to the letter
Halachic	Adj. from halacha
Ha Teva	Nature

Hineini	Here I am; I am present
Hochma(h)	Wisdom; Sacred Feminine in Judaism
Hodesh	Month; moon
Kabbala(h)	Body of teachings of the inner or mystical core of Judaism
Kavanna(h)	Intention, mindfulness
Kairos	Archetypal image used to indicate limitless time
Koan	Buddhist concept of a phrase inaccessible to rational interpretation
Kippah	Head covering, used during prayer
K'rubh	Root for cherub; intermediary between Divinity and humanity
Ketuvim	Section of Bible entitled Writings
L'chaim	The Jewish toast: To Life
Menorah	Seven branched candelabra
Midrash	Story of explanation of biblical text
Midrashic	Adj. from midrash
Midrashim	Plural of midrash
Mikveh	Ritual bath
Minyan	Gathering of ten, traditionally required for prayer
Mishkan	Portable dwelling place for The Divine Presence; tabernacle, tent of meeting; from root shachan
Mitzvot	Commandments, often thought of as good deeds
Namaste	Greeting; I respect the divinity with you that is within me; Sanskrit
Nephilim	Legendary beings; legendary giants
Nevi'im	Section of the Bible entitled The Prophets
Patriarchy	Hierarchical social construct based on favoring the male in society at the

	expense of The Other
Pesach	Festival of Passover
P'shat	Surface or literal reading of biblical text
Rebbetzin	Wife of rabbi
Remez	Hint; allegorical interpretation of biblical text
Responsa	Body of Jewish literature that answers contemporary issues from textual resources
Rosh chodesh	New month; "head of the month"
Rosh Hashan(h)	New Year
Ruach	Breath, spirit
Sangoma	Shaman, of Nguni tribes of South Africa
Seder	Order; usually used for the Passover meal
Sephira	One of the energy sources on the Tree of Life: Keter, Chochmah, Binah, Daat, Chesed, Gevurah, Tiferet, Hod, Netzach, Yesod, Malchut
Sephirot	Plural of sephira
Shabbat	Sabbath
Shalom	Peace; greeting; etymology — completion, wholeness
Shalom bayit	Peace at home: peace in the Jewish community
Shande	Yiddish for scandalous
Shavuot	Pilgrimage summer festival; associated with the Giving of the Law
Shachan	Hebrew verb to dwell among; to settle
Shechina(h)	Indwelling presence; feminine face of God; Sacred Feminine in Judaism
Sh'ma	The Watch Word of Judaism stating that God is One

Shofar	Ram's horn used ritually to spiritually call us to presence
Sod	The hidden meaning of a biblical text
Spirituality	Way of being relating, to The Whole; basis of religious impulse within humankind common to all
Sukkot	Fall festival of Booths, reminding us of the temporary nature of life
Tallit	Prayer shawl
Talmud	Bodies of interpretative work based on Torah; legal authority
Teshuva	Return
Tanach	Bible composed of T Torah (Five Books of Moses) N Nevi'im (Prophets) K Ketuvim (Writings)
Tetragrammaton	The unvocalized name of God, yud-hay-vav-hey,
Torah	Bible comprising Books of Genesis, Exodus, Leviticus, Numbers, Deuteronomy
Tikkun olam	Reparation of the world
Tu B'shvat	New Year of The Trees, celebrated in January/February
Unus mundus	The one world uniting the visible and invisible hidden within it
Yahwe	Vocalized name for the tetragrammaton
Yetzirah	Third world in the kabbalistic framework translated as Formation
Yom HaShoah	The commemoration of the tragedy of the Nazi Holocaust
Yom Kippur	The Day of Atonement

References

Abram, David. *The Spell of The Sensuous: Perception and Language in a More-Than-Human World*, Vintage Books, New York, 1996

Adelman, Penina. *Miriam's Well: Rituals for Jewish Women Around the Year*, Biblio Press, New York, 1986

Bolen, Jean Shinoda. *Urgent Message From Mother: Gather The Women and Save The World*, Conari Press, San Francisco, 2005

Brettler, Marc Z. *How To Read The Bible*, Jewish Publication Society, Philadelphia, 2005

Bryant, Dorothy. *The Kin of Ata Are Waiting For You*, Random House, New York, 1971

Cameron, James: *The Exodus Decoded*, DVD, History Channel, 2006

Childs, Brevard: *Myth and Reality in The Old Testament*, Alec R. Allenson Inc, Florida, 1960

Cooper, David. *God is a Verb: Kabbalah and the Practice of Mystical Judaism*, Riverhead Books, New York, 1998

Diamant, Anita. *The Red Tent*, St. Martin's Press, New York, 1997

Drosnin, Michael. *The Bible Code*, Simon and Shuster, New York, 1997

Eisler, Riane. *The Chalice and the Blade: Our History, Our Future*, Harper Row, San Francisco, 1987

Emoto, Masaru. *The Hidden Messages in Water*, Beyond Words Publishing, Oregon, 2004

Falk, Marcia. *The Book of Blessings*, Beacon Press, Massachusetts, 1996

Friedman, Richard E. *Who Wrote The Bible?* Simon and Schuster Inc, New York, 1987

Gawain, Shakti. *Creative Visualization: Use The Power Of Your Imagination To Create What You Want In Your Life*, New World Library, California, 1978

Gimbutas, Marija. *The Language of the Goddess*, Harper Collins,

New York, 1989

HaLevi, Z'ev Ben Shimon. *Kabbalah and The Exodus*, Rider and Company, United Kingdom, 1980 HaLevi, Z'ev Ben Shimon. *Tree of Life*, Rider and Company, United Kingdom, 1972

HaLevi, Z'ev Ben Shimon. *The Way of Kabbalah*, Rider and Company, United Kingdom, 1975

HaLevi, Z'ev Ben Shimon. *Kabbalah: Tradition of Hidden Knowledge*, Thames and Hudson, United Kingdom, 1979

Howell, Alice O. *The Heaven's Declare: Astrological Age And The Evolution Of Consciousness*, Quest Books, Illinois, 1990

Kidd, Sue Monk. *The Dance Of The Dissident Daughter: A Woman's Journey From The Christian Tradition To The Sacred Feminine*, HarperCollins, New York, 1996

Kramer, Samuel Noah. *History Begins At Sumer: Thirty-Nine Firsts In Recorded History*, University of Pennsylvania Press, Philadelphia, 1956

Kushner, Lawrence. *The River of Light: Spirituality, Judaism and the Evolution of Consciousness*, Jewish Lights, Vermont, 1993

Labowitz, Shoni. *Miraculous Living: A Guided Journey In Kabbalah Through The Ten Gates Of The Tree Of Life*, Simon and Schuster. New York, 1996

Lerner, Michael. *Jewish Renewal: A Path To Healing And Transformation*, Grossett Putnam, NY, 1994

Lew, Alan. *Be Still and Get Going: A Jewish Meditation Practice For Real Life*, Little, Brown and Company, New York, 2005

Manji, Irshad. *The Trouble With Islam: A Muslim's Call For Reform In Her Faith*, St. Martin's Press, New York, 2003

Mendel, Heather: *Towards Freedom: A Feminist Haggadah For Men And Women In The New Millennium*, A Word of Art, California, 1995

Moore, Thomas. *Care of the Soul: A Guide For Cultivating Depth And Sacredness In Everyday Life*, HarperCollins, New York, 1992

Myss, Caroline. *Anatomy Of The Spirit: The Seven Stages Of Power and Healing*, Crown Publishers, New York, 1996

Patai, Raphael. *The Hebrew Goddess*, Wayne State University Press, Michigan, 1967

Piercy, Marge. *He, She and It*, Fawcett, New York, 1993

Plaskow, Judith. *Standing Again At Sinai*, Harper Row, New York,1990

Pearson, Carol. *Awakening The Heroes Within: Twelve Archetypes To Help Us Find Ourselves And Transform the World*, HarperCollins, New York, 1991

Sameth, Mark. *God's Hidden Name Revealed*, Reform Judaism, NY, Spring 2009

Sams, Jamie. *The Thirteen Original Clan Mothers: Your Sacred Path To Discovering The Gifts, Talents And Abilities Of The Feminine*, HarperCollins, New York, 1993

Schaef, Anne Wilson. *Women's Reality: An Emerging Female System In A White Male Society*, HarperCollins, New York, 1981

Schlain, Leonard. *The Alphabet Versus The Goddess: The Conflict Between Word And Image*, Viking, New York, 1998

Shapiro, Rami. *Minyan: Ten Principles For Living A Life Of Integrity*, Bell Tower, New York, 1997

Siegel, Danny. *Unlocked Doors*, Town House Press, New York, 1983

Sitchin, Zecharia. *Genesis Revisted*, Avon, New York, 1990

Stern, Chaim. Editor of *Gates Of Repentance: The New Union Prayerbook For The Days Of Awe*, Central Conference of American Rabbis, New York, 1978

Stern, Chaim. Editor of the *New Union Prayer Book*, adaptation of words by Ralph Waldo Emerson, Central Conference of American Rabbis, New York, 1987

Stone, Merlin. *When God Was A Woman*, Harcourt Brace, Florida, 1976

Sugrue, Thomas. *There Is A River: The Story Of Edgar Cayce*, ARE, Virginia, 2003

Swimme, Brian. *The Hidden Heart Of The Cosmos*, Orbis Books, NY

1996

Teilhard De Chardin, Pierre. *The Phenomenon Of Man*, Harper Row, NY 1959

Taylor, Jeremy. *Dream Work: Techniques For Discovering the Creative Power in Dreams*, Paulist Press, New York, 1983

Teubal, Savina. *Sarah The Priestess: The First Matriarch Of Genesis*, Swallow Press, Ohio, 1984

Tolle, Eckhard: *A New Earth: Awakening To Your Life's Purpose*, Plume, New York, 2006

Velikovsky, Immanuel: *Worlds In Collision*, Gollancz, United Kingdom, 1965

Watson, Lyall. *Supernature*, Anchor Press, United Kingdom,1973

West, John Anthony: *Serpent In The Sky*, Quest Books, Illinois, 1993

Wolf, Fred. *Mind Into Matter: A New Alchemy Of Science And Spirit*, Moment Point press, New Hampshire, 2001

BOOKS

O is a symbol of the world, of oneness and unity. In different cultures it also means the "eye," symbolizing knowledge and insight. We aim to publish books that are accessible, constructive and that challenge accepted opinion, both that of academia and the "moral majority."

Our books are available in all good English language bookstores worldwide. If you don't see the book on the shelves ask the bookstore to order it for you, quoting the ISBN number and title. Alternatively you can order online (all major online retail sites carry our titles) or contact the distributor in the relevant country, listed on the copyright page.

See our website **www.o-books.net** for a full list of over 500 titles, growing by 100 a year.

And tune in to myspiritradio.com for our book review radio show, hosted by June-Elleni Laine, where you can listen to the authors discussing their books.

MySpiritRadio